Raising Your Daughter From Ages 0-10: A Complete Handbook for Dads

A Month-by-Month Look At What to Expect, Developmental Tips & Ideas For Activities

By:
Jenn Greenleaf

The sale of this book without its cover is unauthorized. If you purchased this book without a cover, you should be aware it was reported to the distributor as "unsold or destroyed." Neither the author nor the publisher has received payment for the sale of this "stripped book."

Copyright © 2010 by Jennifer Greenleaf

All rights reserved. No Year of this book may be reproduced or transmitted in any form or by any means without prior written permission from the author, except for the inclusion of brief quotations in a review.

ISBN: 1453706712
EAN-13: 9781453706718

First printing July 2010

Cover design: Jennifer Greenleaf

Printed in the U.S.A.

*This book is dedicated to Chris,
Brett Jr., Larisa, and Michael with much love.*

Preface:

What Have I Gotten Myself Into?!

"A father is always making his baby into a little woman. And when she is a woman he turns her back again." -- Enid Bagnold

Welcome to the wonderful world of fatherhood! You're probably looking at this book for one reason: because you're completely freaked out about being a dad to a daughter and you seriously need some help because you don't know where else to turn! Okay, it doesn't have to be quite that dramatic. However, it is not uncommon for new dads to feel that way and seek guidance. You've come to the right place! This book is a quick, no nonsense handbook for your daughter's first ten years.

You will likely be feeling with conflicting emotions you will inevitably have to deal with. Prior to the birth of your daughter, thoughts of "oh my god, what am I going to do," will float through your mind randomly, but don't let them control you! There are ways to battle these emotions and resolve them.

First, figure out what could be contributing to these conflicting emotions. Ask yourself the following questions:

1. Is it financial stress? This is a common source of stress, but it's manageable. If you're facing temporary loss of income, then focus on that. If you're facing the loss of income due to the loss of a second paycheck, plan for this loss well in advance.

2. Are you afraid you're going to feel like a third wheel? It's difficult for some dads to go from being the center of attention to hitting the sidelines. This is normal and it is also manageable.

3. Do you fear there will be losing your love life? Even though it feels like romance and intimacy are lost forever, they're not despite this new addition. Be patient.

4. Will there be changes in relationships? There's a huge change in the family dynamics, including how needs are met for each other. Be prepared for that.

5. How much will lifestyles be altered? The need and desire to stay home to care for and adjust to your daughter will become a reality. This is troublesome for some fathers with full social calendars.

6. Am I going to suffer from sleep deprivation? If you're not careful, sleep deprivation can cause forms of depression. This is manageable, though. Be prepared for frequent waking because it is inevitable.

Next, figure out how to resolve these conflicting emotions. There are a number of ways you can do so, but the number one way is to become as actively involved in fathering as possible. Here are some tips:

- If your work schedule permits, ask if you can "room-in" with your daughter and her mother until it's time for them to return home.

- Be involved as much as possible from the very beginning in order to prevent you from feeling like a babysitter.

- Create an emotional bond right from the start by allowing yourself to be a key participant in the very early stages of her life.

This book is broken down into quick, easy to consume chunks of information that will help you understand what to expect, how to help your daughter with development, and give you ideas for activities to do together. You'll be able to flip through this book on a month-to-month basis for quick glances into helping you raise your daughter. It's not going to be easy, but it will be fun!

Real Life Reflections: "Your child's behavior is your indicator of their well-being. The behavior is your clue, your signal to the internal emotional state that lies beneath the behavior and triggers it – even the awful, annoying, embarrassing, exhausting behavior. It's what tells you how your child is doing. Be grateful for it. It's all you have to let you know what your child needs. What she doesn't have is words and an understanding of what is going on – it's all there in her behavior. You just have to put your detective hat on to uncover the cause.

Adults are quite capable of keeping their internal emotions under wrap, but children are raw – thank goodness. They don't know yet how to keep a lid on it. What specifically is generating the behavior may not be apparent. It's not always necessary to know. What is necessary – what makes all the difference in how we handle the behavior – is the perception that the behavior you see is rooted in something real – a deeper emotional state." – Bonnie Harris is author of *Confident Parents, Remarkable Kids: 8 Principles for Raising Kids You'll Love to Live With* (Adams Media, Sept. 2008), and wrote the parenting classic, *When Kids Push Your Buttons* (Warner Books), a top-selling title that has been translated into a half a dozen languages. She's an esteemed parenting educator, international speaker, and a pioneer of child behavior strategies.

Raising Your Daughter from Ages 0-10

Year One:

Look Here, I Need Help Getting Through the First Year!

"To a father growing old nothing is dearer than a daughter." -- Euripides

Crib Notes:

- Just because you have a girl, that doesn't mean all the diapering should be left to her mother. Get your hands dirty, Daddy!

- Be involved as much as possible from day one to establish a bond right away – don't worry, you won't break her!

- Don't panic each time you hear her cry – it will be okay!

Month one:

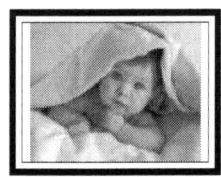

"Daughters are like flowers, they fill the world with beauty, and sometimes attract pests." -- Author Unknown

What to Expect:

- Your daughter's umbilical cord stump should fall off between one and three weeks. The nurse or your daughter's pediatrician should supply you with information about cord care while you're all still in the hospital.

- Some babies start making "baby noises," and some laugh a little during their first four weeks.

- Your daughter may try holding your gaze when you attempt to make eye contact with her.

Developmental Tips:

- Let your daughter set the pace for feeding from day one, and support the baby's mother in these efforts as much as possible.

- Watch your daughter for comfort patterns, such as sleep patterns, that will trigger your ability to care for her better.

- Purchase a front-wearing sling or baby carrier that you can strap to yourself and hold your baby with to further enable the two of you to bond.

Ideas For Activities:

- Hold your daughter as much as possible to help with the bonding process.

- Be goofy, make funny faces, and laugh a lot when changing your daughter!

- Playing pass: You will not actually be throwing and expecting your daughter to throw back. Instead, you will be handing an item back and forth. You will need a small toy or a ball. Pas the item back and forth with your daughter explaining what you are doing. Why? This activity teaches hand-eye coordination, as well as communication of "my space" and "your space."

 **Real Life Reflections:** "My youngest screamed bloody murder in her car seat, from birth until about two months. We finally bought a CD of ocean sounds and that helped, but it took a couple of months before she really got comfortable with it. A few times she got so hysterical we had to pull over and take her out of her seat until she calmed down." - December Quinn

Month two:

"The love of a father is one of nature's greatest masterpieces." -- Unknown

What to Expect:

- Your daughter may develop "cradle cap," which is a harmless film accompanied by red bumps. It will go away on its own.

- Her nails are going to grow quickly and they're going to be sharp enough to scratch her, so be sure to trim them often with nail scissors to keep the edges blunt.

- Frequent watery stools may become routine, but that doesn't mean it is diarrhea or that you should be concerned. If it's watery, consult her pediatrician.

Developmental Tips:

- Hold your daughter close during bottle-feeding, but don't prop the bottle up on a pillow so you can do something else – be present in the moment to further bond with your baby.

- Place your daughter on her side and see if she can roll to her back. If she can't, move her in that direction to give her the opportunity to make this discovery with help.

- Help your daughter develop soothing techniques by swaddling her after baths, comforting her, and making it an enjoyable experience. Some babies find bathing frightening, so this helps develop gentle feelings in this regard.

Ideas For Activities:

- Take lots of pictures and, either put them into photo albums (label them!) or use them in scrapbooks (yes, some dads DO scrapbook!).

- Take lots of videos and, if you keep the date stamp on the screen, you should be able to number them consecutively to keep them in order.

- Peek-a-Boo Pillow: Find a pillow and a soft blanket for this activity. Lay your daughter on the soft blanket on her back. Lean over her and, with the pillow hiding your face, engage in a game of peek-a-boo.

Real Life Reflections: "My daughter suffered from serious reflux as an infant. After each meal we got into the habit of keeping her propped up with pillows (those triangle pillows are fantastic) to reduce the chances of food coming back up." - Rebecca Laffar-Smith

Month three:

"Blessed indeed is the man who hears many gentle voices call him father!" -- Lydia M. Child

What to Expect:

- Your daughter may have enough strength in her arms and her neck to lift herself when lying face down.

- She will enjoy discovering her hands and her reflection in mirrors.

- You may notice your daughter reaching out and grabbing objects in front of her or near her more often.

Developmental Tips:

- As soon as your daughter develops head control, start laying her on her belly from time to time to help develop her arm and neck muscles further.
- Interact with her as much as possible because, at this age, it has been noted that frequent stimulation and interaction is as important as feeding your baby and her sleep routine.
- Try to phase out nighttime feedings by spreading out feedings as much as possible to encourage longer periods of uninterrupted sleep.

Ideas For Activities:

- Write your thoughts down in a journal or in the blocks of a calendar as your daughter continues to grow, change, and develop right before your eyes.

- Make a mobile: This activity is more for your daughter, than one you will engage in with her. Gather the following materials: embroidery hoop or pie tin, heavyweight string, assorted household objects, stuffed animals, and ceiling hook. Hang each of the items from the embroidery hook or pie tin and, to add sparkle, add assorted cut from cardboard and covered over with tin foil.

- Read aloud: There's no doubt you're going to be filled with questions during the first few weeks following the birth of your daughter. Because she's still so little, she's not going to be very interested in doing much more than eating or sleeping most of the time. When researching your new role as a father, read out loud to your daughter. This information can be from books, magazines, and the Internet. Your daughter won't care what you're reading at this point. However, she will be interested in the soothing sound of your voice.

Real Life Reflections: "When my daughter (who is now two and a half) was about three months old my wife and I would have trouble trying to get her to nap during the day. When I would get home from work, I would sit on the armchair and let her lay, with her head on my chest, and she would fall asleep within moments. My wife tried this to no avail. Only happened with me and I was thus dubbed 'the Daddy mattress.' Although, the obvious reason here is my wife was breast-feeding and if she tried to settle her, Hazel (my daughter) could obviously smell the milk. So I was cheated by not breast-feeding her!" – J. Leslie Voss, Australia

Month four:

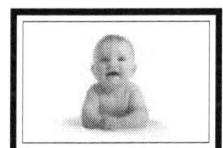

"Noble fathers have noble children." -- Euripides

What to Expect:

- Expect your daughter to be very active and alert during feedings and, because of this activity it may be difficult to keep the bottle in her mouth at times.

- Your daughter may sleep longer periods of time by now. Some parents have reported up to nine hours of solid sleep on some nights.

- She will start repeating vowel sounds, as well as make these sounds during spontaneous baby babble.

Developmental Tips:

- Help encourage speech development by coaxing your daughter to repeat vowel sounds and other sounds.
- Start introducing solid foods gradually this month to help develop swallowing muscles and learn new flavors, but don't go too fast or else your daughter will not absorb adequate calories for proper growth.
- Pick brightly colored toys (babies seem to prefer primary colors) to help your daughter develop interests, curiosities, and preferences. Be sure these toys are very similar to one another to further develop exploration of new things.

Ideas For Activities:

- Have a family portrait taken.

- Take her hand and foot prints by rubbing poster paint on the palms or her hands and the bottoms of her feet (one at a time, of course) and pressing them on to poster board (don't forget to put the date!).

- Splish-Splash! It's probably already become apparent to you that your daughter, like most babies, love to play in the water. All you'll need for this activity is brightly colored bath time toys. Encourage your daughter to push the toys around, make them sink, and splash them around. Spend some time pushing the toys around, as well, and encourage her to chase your toys with her toys.

Real Life Reflections: "When my oldest was a baby I played around with familiar tunes and new lyrics. One is sung to the tune of Jesus Loves Me, but I altered the words to apply to Mommy or Daddy (or whomever). In case your targeted dads would be interested in this sort of thing, here's my phrasing:

Daddy loves you, yes he does,
Daddy loves you very much,
Little one whom he adores,
You are his and he is yours,
Yes, Daddy loves you,
Yes, Daddy loves you,
Yes, Daddy loves you,
He cold not love you more.

The mental picture of a daddy singing this to his little girl melts my heart." – Janna Qualman

Month five:

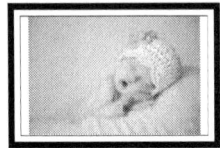

"The joys of parents are secret, and so are their griefs and fears." -- Francis Bacon, Sr.

What to Expect:

- Your daughter will still be very interested in napping several times throughout the day, but may show resistance to falling asleep sometimes and may not sleep for as long.

- Colic should be a thing of the past by now, despite afternoon fussiness and other bouts of unexplained crying.

- Additional safety precautions must be in place because your daughter is going to be very wiggly on the changing table and explorative in her crib.

Developmental Tips:

- Introduce new foods about every seven days to better determine which foods might be causing an allergic reaction.
- Encourage reaching and turning by holding toys close up to your daughter and then moving the toys away to further challenge her.
- Because infection-fighting antibodies have pretty much dissipated by this month, your daughter will need help preventing colds and bacterial infections. Avoid coming into contact with those who are sick, or those who have just gotten over a virus.

Ideas For Activities:

- Where did it go? This activity will enhance skills with curiosity, as well as concentration. Show your daughter a toy and encourage her to pass it between her hands and yours. Then, drop it and see if she tries to find where it went, p-repeat this game as long as she's interested.

- Set up a play date with cousins that might be in her age group.

- Bring your daughter on a field trip to visit Grandma and Grandpa.

 **Real Life Reflections:** "When my now nine year old was born . . . After kicking my ribs for the previous four months, giving me morning sickness any 'ol time of day from day one until about two months before she was born and heartburn that would have brought a grown man to tears nearly every day of the entire pregnancy, my girl was born six days late and was handed to me red faced and screaming. No amount of cooing and kisses from Mommy did anything to quiet my little angel girl. BUT – the nurse handed her to her Daddy and instantly the howling princess stopped screaming, looked up at her Daddy's face, and I kid you not, cooed at him. She's been Daddy's girl ever since. As a matter of fact, he's taken her to her ballet class at the moment, and they have a go cart in the garage they're building." – LaurieD, AbsoluteWrite.com forums

Month six:

"A daughter is the happy memories of the past, the joyful moments of the present, and the hope and promise of the future." -- Author Unknown

What to Expect:

- Your daughter might start growing at a more rapid rate by now, if she hasn't already, giving her a pudgy appearance.

- She may show resistance (or full blown tantrums) when it comes to being transitioned out of the baby tub and into a full sized tub. Do this gradually because it is normal for babies this age to dislike full-sized tubs.

- You might notice your daughter being able to sit up briefly without help, but she may still prefer lying on her back and sucking on her toes.

Developmental Tips:

- Drop a toy or another object to encourage her to look for them once they are out of her sight.

- Encourage your daughter to reach out whenever she wants to be picked up to give her indication that you understand her emotional cues.

- Gradually introduce your daughter to new people to increase her ability to self-sooth and alleviate feelings of unwariness around strangers.

Ideas For Activities:

- Mirror Magic: Sit on the floor with your daughter in your lap in front of a mirror. Tough your daughter's head, eyes, nose and chin, naming each as you go. Sing these body Years to make it more fun for you and your daughter. Make funny faces and encourage her to do the same.

- Get some blank keys to play with her with from the hardware store.

- Get some fabric books that make noises and have interesting textures to play with her with.

 **Real Life Reflections:** "Don't believe the published milestones. There were any number of books and magazine articles that said my daughter should be potty trained by eighteen months, that she should talk at this time, and walk at that time. Not true and I have dozens of examples to prove it. She was way earlier on some and later on others. Your child is your child. Your doctor will identify any real issue and work with you on them." – Jason, Georgia

Month seven:

"You don't really understand human nature unless you know why a child on a merry-go-round will wave at his

Raising Your Daughter from Ages 0-10

parents every time around - and why his parents will always wave back." -- William D. Tammeus

What to Expect:

- Your daughter might start trying to crawl around by pulling her upper body up, and then dragging her belly and legs behind.

- She will start using her sense of taste to explore new objects more and more, including toys (and everything else, for that matter).

- You might notice your daughter pulling herself into a standing position while leaning against heavyweight furniture like couches and chairs.

Developmental Tips:

- Help your daughter gradually accept what is strange to her (new voices, new smells, new sounds, new environments, etc.) by soothing her and showing her how comfortable you are with this source of her anxiety.

- Develop your daughter's insatiable need to explore by baby-proofing your home and doing daily safety inspections to ensure she can be curious without being in harm's way.

- Further develop your daughter's hand to mouth skills by offering her pieces of cereal, peas, cut up fruits, cut up vegetables, noodles, and bread.

Ideas For Activities:

- Painted Prints:
  - Get a variety of poster, tempera, or finger-paints and put some of each color on separate paper plates.
  - Set out pieces of paper, or a roll or paper unrolled a little.
  - Using a sponge brush, tickle the bottoms of your daughter's feet with paint.
  - Press her feet on to the paper and show her the surprise.
- Continue reading aloud to your daughter.
- Start coloring with her even if you're the one doing all the work, she'll still enjoy watching you.

Real Life Reflections: "When my daughter was around six or seven months old, we started her on vegetables that were not from the jar. She hated green beans with a passion and made the funniest face – I had to take pictures while my wife attempted to feed her. She liked cubes of carrots, though, so it wasn't a Kodak moment that time." – Anthony, Portland, Oregon

Month eight:

"Making the decision to have a child is momentous. It is to decide forever to have your heart go walking around outside your body." -- Elizabeth Stone

What to Expect:

- You daughter should be starting to hold objects with a "mitten grasp" when picking up objects.

- Sleep patterns could see up to ten or eleven hours of uninterrupted sleep, and some parents have noted that their babies are only awake about nine hours out of the day when naps are taken into consideration.

- You'll probably notice your daughter listening to you more intently and understanding a lot more words than in previous months.

Developmental Tips:

- Repeat a lot (or all of) the sounds and syllables your daughter makes to further prepare for speech.

- Demonstrate new toys to your daughter to help her understand how they work, and further develop her skills for "paying attention."

- Sit your daughter down on the floor and encourage her to sit on her own for longer periods of time. Don't make her over-tired, though, or else she'll be more discouraged than anything else.

Ideas For Activities:

- Go for a naming walk: Take your daughter for a walk around your neighborhood. Be sure she's not leaning too far back in her stroller so she understands that you're talking to her. Point to and name as much as you can as you pass by. Be sure she's looking at where you're pointing. Pay attention to what interests and excites her.

- Bring your daughter grocery shopping and name everything you put into the cart.

- Bring her to the playground to watch how other kids play, and let her wiggle around on a very big blanket.

Real Life Reflections: "When we were teaching my daughter to sit on her own, we would yell TIMBER every time she fell over so she would laugh instead of cry. It worked like a charm! She spent more time laughing about her falls than crying about them. Whenever we didn't yell TIMBER, though, she seemed confused and would fuss. She paid more attention than we gave her credit for." – Rich, Portsmouth, New Hampshire

Month nine:

"Always kiss your children goodnight - even if they're already asleep." -- H. Jackson Brown, Jr.

What to Expect:

- Don't be surprised if she all of a sudden starts showing resistance when you put her in her crib, or leave her alone in a playpen.

- Your daughter will probably start using furniture more often to pull herself up into a standing position and pull herself along.

- You may notice your daughter doing things to get a positive reaction from you and her mother a lot more often.

Developmental Tips:

- Help you daughter with separation anxieties, which are typical for this age, by introducing her gradually to babysitters by keeping the sessions very short at first.

- Your daughter will likely be teething by now, so help her through the process by giving her hard things to bite down on, giving her teething biscuits, and rubbing her gums to sooth them with a gauze wrapped finger.

- Keep board books, activity boards, and games that come apart (pop apart beads, stacking rings, stacking cubes, etc.) to develop thinking and problem solving skills.

Ideas For Activities:

- Big and small: Gather two like items that are different sizes (in other words, a big plastic cup and a small plastic cup, a big ball and a small ball). Gather a variety and place them in front of your daughter. Each time she picks something up, explain to her if it's big or small. "That's a big sock," or, "that's a small book." Take turns picking things up with her and continue explaining big and small.

- Separate colored wooden blocks out in front of your daughter and see how she reacts to this type of sorting.

- Separate colored blocks by shape, rather than color, and see how your daughter reacts to that type of sorting.

Real Life Reflections: "My daughter is adopted from China. We were lucky to have her join our family when she was nine months old. She is now eight.

During the adoption preparation, social workers warned us there might be issues when she realized she did not look like us, and they were right. It nearly broke my heart when she came home on day and told me she didn't like the way shoe looked, and she wished I was Chinese too. I have always told her how pretty she is, but the comment that had the most effect on her was from dad. She came to me one night after she had helped her brush the tangles from her hair and said, 'Daddy says I have beautiful hair!' Somehow it meant so much coming from him. Here's a poem she wrote for school (it supposed to be in cinquain form):

Dad
Nice, Carrying me,
Helps me much
I love you much
Daddy" – Melia, Ohio

Month ten:

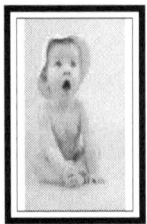

"Before I got married I had six theories about bringing up children; now I have six children, and no theories." -- John Wilmot

What to Expect:

- You may hear your daughter saying at least one word, or something that sounds like a word, by now.

- She might be ready to drink from a sippy cup by now.

- You'll likely notice a response like crying or visible distress when your daughter is scolded by you or her mother for doing something that is a "no-no."

Developmental Tips:

- If you have the room in your kitchen place pots, pans, measuring cups, plastic mixing spoons, mixing bowls, and other kitchen items reserved specifically for your daughter to discover, play with, and nest one inside each other.

- Because your daughter is more mobile, there will be a greater urgency to baby proof your home. That way, you're keeping her safe and you're not stifling her development.

- Help your daughter develop speech by naming everything you touch, anything you hand to her, anything she touches, or anything she hands to you. These familiar objects will soon have a "name" in her mind, and she'll begin to vocalize these familiar names.

Ideas For Activities:

- If your daughter enjoys the large bathtub, make shapes in the bubbles with her.

- Go fly a kite! Even if she's sitting in her stroller, she'll enjoy seeing the kite in flight.

- Catch the Bubbles:

    o Bring some bubbles outside with your daughter.

    o Set her on the grass in front of your and blow some bubbles so they go passed her to the left of right.

o Encourage her to crawl after them and catch them.

Real Life Reflections: "I'm a breastfeeding mother, (baby led feeding, to boot. No timetables in this house.) and both pf my girls (three and ten months), are total daddy's girls. He bathes, changes, cuddles, tosses them around, flips them around and has a football hold he does with them, with back pat, that knocks them right out when they are having a hard time getting to sleep for a nap. How we did that was, when they were wee babies, and had nice full tummies and were all sleepy, he took them and cuddled them down to sleep, several times a day. He did that whenever he was home with them. I got to eat, shower, do chores, nap, while he had some daddy time. he also did a lot of baby-wearing. Both girls often fell asleep on him, after they had been fed. Doing that helps give mom a break, gives dad bonding time and teaches the children that *both* parents are a source of comfort, right from the start." – Megan, Australia

Month eleven:

"To bring up a child in the way he should go, travel that way yourself once in a while." -- Josh Billings

What to Expect:

- She'll likely be creeping and crawling on her hands and knees now, rather than pulling her body with her arms.
- She might start standing alone without falling.
- You might notice that she's able to pull things out that are stuck into tight places, especially when it something you thought was tucked safely out of her reach.

Developmental Tips:

- Help your daughter develop confidence in her abilities to start walking by giving her something sturdy to walk against, like a play shopping cart.
- Continue helping your daughter develop a vocabulary through repetitive play. Repeat whatever sounds she makes, and encourage her to repeat whatever you're saying.

- Give your daughter foods cut or chopped very small, rather than mashing it up like in previous months, to help her develop the ability to feed herself.

Ideas For Activities:

- Continue to take lots and lots of pictures (and label the pictures!).
- Continue to take lots and lots of videos (and continue to number the tapes in order).
- Teach Your Child About Colors and Matching:
    - Take out a blue and green piece of construction paper.
    - Find blocks the same colors.
    - Build with the blocks with your daughter while they're all mixed up, and name the color of each block you pick up, and name the color of each block you use.
    - Build using all the same colors, again naming each color of each block as they're used.
    - Ask your daughter to building using the blue blocks on its matching piece of paper. Repeat this using the green blocks.

- Play this game consistently to develop and reinforce color matching techniques and skills.

> **Real Life Reflections:** "He's been working two jobs and a lot of hours, and he's concerned about the small amount of interaction he has with them (his daughters). He knows how crucial a father's presence is for girls (for the esteem, for their development), and how impressionable they are when small. That being the case, he makes that much more effort when they are together." – Janna, AbsoluteWrite.com forums

Month twelve:

"Your children need your presence more than your presents." -- Jesse Jackson

What to Expect:

- She'll likely start exercising her larger muscles by bouncing or being a lot more active, rather than working on her gross motor skills further.

- Your daughter's attention span will probably grow during independent play as her interests and curiosities continue to develop.

- You'll notice a new side to your daughter, which some consider destructive, because she'll enjoy knocking things down, dumping things out, and turning things over . . . even if these things are not her own toys!

Developmental Tips:

- Further help your daughter enhance her walking skills by choosing shoes that are lightweight and flexible.
- Start developing your daughter's sense of mealtime by always keeping her at the table with you during mealtime, and by showing her that

- she's eating food that is the same (or similar) to what you're eating.

- Help your daughter further develop her palette by re-introducing foods that she has rejected previously because her tastes will change quickly.

Ideas For Activities:

- Continue coloring with your daughter, even if she's just scribbling – scribbling helps her figure out how to hold the crayons.

- Start some basic counting with her by asking for one crayon, and then asking for two crayons and so on.

- Create a Color Collection:

    o Take a laundry basket or, if your daughter has one, a play shopping cart.

    o Go from room to room asking your daughter to find one item of a certain color for in each room you go into.

    o Affirm her selection by saying, "Yes, that's jut like the yellow banana you found in the kitchen."

    o Repeat this game using all the primary colors.

Real Life Reflections: "When my daughter (who's now nearly eight) was about a year old and we took her off formula to put her on milk, she wanted nothing to do with milk. Wouldn't drink it at all. Then I started spiking it with vanilla extract. It worked like a charm and I could decrease the amount of vanilla until we got to the point where she didn't miss it when I stopped putting it in." – Kimberly Nee

Year Two:

Learning New Stages and Changes

"A daughter is a gift of love." -- Author Unknown

Crib Notes:

- Just because there are other girls you know her age that are potty trained already, that doesn't mean there's something wrong with your daughter if she's not.

- Expose your daughter to your interests at an early age to help avoid gender stereotypical activities, as she grows older.

- Don't be afraid to play "girlie" things with her – she's not going to go to her mom every time she wants to play with make-up. Get ready for some glitter, Daddy!

Month thirteen:

Raising Your Daughter from Ages 0-10

"The father of a daughter is nothing but a high-class hostage. A father turns a stony face to his sons, berates them, shakes his antlers, paws the ground, snorts, runs them off into the underbrush, but when his daughter puts her arm over his shoulder and says, "Daddy, I need to ask you something," he is a pat of butter in a hot frying pan." -- Garrison Keillor

What to Expect:

- Don't be surprised if your daughter is very interested in riding toys that have no pedals over any other toy as she becomes more active.

- It may appear that your daughter has no appetite, but this is normal so don't push her to eat more than she wants to or finish what is in front of her.

- She's going to likely do whatever she can to keep herself awake because she's not going to want to miss what's happening around her or elsewhere in the household.

Developmental Tips:

- Help your daughter explore new textures and develop new tastes at the dinner table by introducing several different kinds of foods during mealtime (like something creamy, something crunchy, and something dry in the same meal).

- Help your daughter get to bed at night easier by establishing a bedtime routine now and stick to it despite how active the household may be in the evenings.

- Developing coping skills is very important and can be done by giving her a special blanket or stuffed animal to sooth herself with during times of stress or separation.

Ideas For Activities:

- Push cars and trucks around in front of her to see if she will do this with you.

- Try teaching her how to pull apart large Duplo blocks.

- Teaching About Sounds:
    o Sit your daughter on your lap or in front of you on the floor.

    o Start making repeating vowel sounds over and over, like a-a-a in different pitches.

- Change the vowel sounds and look for a reaction from your daughter. This is an indication that she's paying attention.
- Ask your daughter to repeat these sounds.

Real Life Reflections: "My daughter turned two in June, and has always been a bit of a daddy's girl. This worked well for us because I was breastfeeding so already has my built-in baby time, so it was nice that she always really enjoyed time with him, too. He has always been very hands-on, diaper changing, late-night rocking, down on the floor playing kind of dad.

We're finding this age interesting as up till now most of her toys have been gender-neutral infant stuff, and now we're getting into more of the dolls versus truck stuff. We don't try to guide her preferences and right now she's at a place where she will happily don a tutu and a hockey helmet while driving her Barbie in a toy backhoe to the fishin' hole. She can name about a dozen different kinds of trucks and tractors, and loves ballerinas and fairies. I think there was a point where my husband had some concerns about whether he could have the kind of relationship with a little girl that he might have had with a son, but it becomes more and more obvious every day that it's not about a father and a daughter. It's about these two specific people and the indescribable depth of love they have for each other.

As we learn this parent thing, we've both discovered some new skills we had no idea we had – for him we've learned he is brilliant at making up one-the-spot words to songs that actually rhyme, unfailingly asks just the right questions to

> extract the information we need ("but where was the butterfly *before* it was in your mouth?") and makes the world's best scrambled eggs and cheese." – Elladog, AbsoluteWrite.com forums

Month fourteen:

"It's not only children who grow. Parents do too. As much as we watch to see what our children do with their lives, they are watching us to see what we do with ours. I can't tell my children to reach for the sun. All I can do is reach for it, myself." -- Joyce Maynard

What to Expect:

- If your daughter uses a pacifier, she may start losing interest in it or, conversely, she may need help weaning from it gradually.

- You might notice your daughter imitating animal sounds, as well as speaking additional words beyond "mamma," and "da-da."

- She'll start expressing a lot of interest in coloring and scribbling on paper during independent, as well as during one on one playtime.

Developmental Tips:

- Help your daughter form shapes and develop the ability to handle crayons better by using large chunky crayons that are easy for her to hold and use.

- Your daughter's confidence will further develop when you lead her as she walks.

- Continuously give her simple commands to help her develop the ability to listen to, and understand simple directions.

Ideas For Activities:

- Try attempting to build with Lincoln Logs.

- Try attempting to build with Tinker toys (the very large plastic kind).

- Develop Problem Solving Skills With Cups:

  o Gather a variety of cups, some the same size and others in different sizes.

- Nest the cups into each other, and then take them back aYear. Ask your daughter to copy you.

- Place these cups next to the other cups that are different sizes to see how your daughter will experiment.

Real Life Reflections: "I have a fourteen month old daughter and I've learned that when getting her to bed at night if something works one night its not a guarantee that it's going to work the next." – Brandy, from Virginia

Month fifteen:

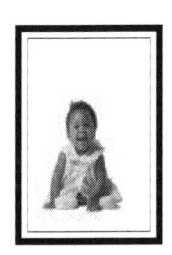

"Don't worry that children never listen to you; worry that they are always watching you." -- Robert Fulghum

What to Expect:

Raising Your Daughter from Ages 0-10   49

- She'll be able to get objects that you name, but she probably won't be able to say them.

- Expect a lot of extra hugs and kisses.

- She may start exploring areas of the home where you are not present.

Developmental Tips:

- Help with her development of language by naming each object that she hands to you or shows you.

- Further develop comfort and security by showing her affection as often as possible.
- Further develop gross motor skills by lying your daughter on her back and encourage her to press her feet against your hands.

Ideas For Activities:

- Go around the house looking for how many there are of things. For example, how many clocks are there? Or, how many things are hanging from the walls? How many pillows are there? And so on...

- When your daughter is eating finger food, count how many of each piece of food there is. For example, how many pieces of cereal does she have? Or, how many crackers are there? And so on...

- Encourage your daughter to count how many red blocks are in a pile, how many blue blocks there are and so on.

Real Life Reflections: "I've got one daughter (and two sons, ages eight and five). She's two and a half years old now. When we brought our daughter home from the hospital, she wanted nothing to do with anyone except Mommy. She didn't even want to look at Daddy. It wasn't until she was closer to four to five months that she realized 'Daddy can be fun, too.'

Our daughter hated the bath from the first moment she entered the water. I thought it was just something she would do for the first time and then she'd love it the next. I was wrong. She screamed like we were killing her every single time for six months. And then one day, she loved it. For the next couple of months, she'd laugh and play in the tub, having a grand time. Then she switched again. She hated it so much that my husband and I took turns taking her in the shower with us. We learned an interesting lesson in this. Little girls can be wishy-washy.

She's very interesting in being a 'mommy.' She loves dolls and loves to share her food, which is very cute. She can count to ten but she still doesn't know all of her colors. She is slightly more dramatic than her brothers. You know, everything's a big event.

She is a little more shy than her brothers and slower to warm up to strangers. I actually have relatives that live out of state (and visit irregularly) that she won't say more than two words to. The other day, I was on the phone with my aunt and DD was talking to me. My aunt couldn't believe it was her! ." – Kristy26, AbosulteWrite.com forums

Month sixteen:

"It behooves a father to be blameless if he expects his child to be." – Homer

What to Expect:

- Your daughter might be able to feed herself with a spoon by now.

- When you're playing with your daughter, she might be able to stack more than just two blocks at a time.

- If she's around stairs, she might be able to climb up them (but will get stuck, so be prepared to be nearby when she attempts this on her own).

Developmental Tips:

- Avoid putting your daughter to bed while she is already asleep, otherwise you're stifling her ability to self-sooth and fall asleep on her own. Relax her to the point of nearly being asleep, and then put her to bed (prepare for resistance).

- Use cookie cutters to create interesting shapes for foods you think your daughter may have difficulty developing a palette for upon sight.

- Help your daughter develop puzzle-building strategies by starting her off with pieces that have handles.

Ideas For Activities:

- Start playing very basic games with your daughter, like Hide and Seek.

- Bring your daughter to the playground and help her on the slide in addition to pushing her in the toddler safety swing.

- Make Some Disposable Blocks to Develop Fine Motor Skills:
  - Save aside empty food boxes in several different sizes. Pasta, rice, oatmeal, and cereal boxes offer a good variety.

- Tape the ends together securely, and cover them over "gift wrap style" using contact paper or construction paper.
- Ask your daughter to decorate the blocks using stickers, paint, and crayons.
- Stack the blocks, counting them as you go.
- Knock your tower down, and ask your daughter to build a tower like you did. Count as she builds.
- Ask her to knock it down and rebuild it higher.
- You will notice the towers getting taller and taller as her fine motor skills continue to develop.

Real Life Reflections: "I love it when I'm taking a nap on the couch and, out of nowhere, I feel my little girl crawling up on to me and falling asleep on my back." – Kyle, Edison, New Jersey

Month seventeen:

"If you have never been hated by your child you have never been a parent." -- Bette Davis

What to Expect:

- Growth will begin to slow considerably during the second year in comparison to her first, so don't be alarmed if she's consistently not putting on weight or growing as quickly.

- Your daughter's likes and dislikes are going to change from week to week, sometimes day to day, so expect her to reject something she previously liked.

- She may develop a food allergy, so be sure to introduce new foods slowly and spaced out so you can tell which foods are causing the rashes, hives, eczema, and other similar reactions.

Developmental Tips:

- Help your daughter develop positive mealtime experiences by keeping the mood peaceful, and avoid power struggles over what she is eating or how much she is eating.

- Praise your daughter each time she attempts to feed herself using utensils in order to help her develop confidence in her abilities.

- Be firm about spitting food or throwing food right from the beginning to help your daughter develop early table manners.

Ideas For Activities:

- Show your daughter how food-coloring changes water with just one drop.

- If weather permits, start teaching your daughter how to make simple sand castles.

- Rolling to Teach Coordination:

    o Your daughter loves moving and being on the go quite a bit by this time, so she'll immediately want to copy you when she sees you rolling on the floor.

    o Ask her to lie on the floor next to you and follow you as you roll from one end of the room to the other.
    o Encourage her to roll on both sides of her body.

- This game is so much fun she'll want to play it with you a lot.

Real Life Reflections: "I have two daughters, ages six and one and a half. One thing I have noticed with both of them is that in the first eighteen months or so they will always go to mommy for cuddles and boo boo healing. As they have gotten older, they have gone to daddy, as well. I'm just now noticing my youngest now being willing to snuggle up with daddy as much as me." – MissKris, AbsoluteWrite.com forums

Month eighteen:

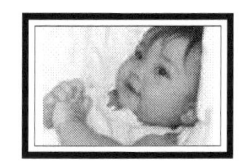

"Certain is it that there is no kind of affection so purely angelic as of a father to a daughter. In love to our wives there is desire; to our sons, ambition; but to our daughters there is something which there are no words to express." -- Joseph Addison

What to Expect:

- Some toddlers still resist bath time; so don't be surprised if she's not the type of child who doesn't want to play in the tub right away.

- You're going to have trouble getting your daughter to sleep, so coming up with positive routines and helping your daughter calm down her imagination is imperative.

- Your daughter is going to try pushing to sleep with you and her mother because she's afraid or insecure.

Developmental Tips:

- Your daughter needs to develop good dental habits early on; otherwise her permanent teeth will be affected, so start now if you haven't already.

- Help your daughter calm down at night be avoiding tickle-time, rough-housing, and other activities that would wind her up like a top.

- The feeling of independence is something that is developed from a very early age, and then reaffirmed by you when you avoid letting her sleep in your bed at night.

Ideas For Activities:

- Get one of those colorful plastic linking chains and encourage her to take them apart, put them together, and attaché different toys to the links.

- Teach your daughter about sizes by giving her nesting bowls that have been taken apart and see if she can nest them back together.

- Tear Paper to Develop Fine Motor Skills:
    o Find an old magazine you know no one in the household is interested in anymore.
    o Tear a page out with bold colors and interesting pictures.
    o Hand the page to your daughter, talk about what is on the page, and ask her to tear up the page.
    o Put the torn pieces into an empty cereal box or oatmeal can.
    o Pour the torn pieces out of the container and ask your daughter to hold her hands out to be tickled by the confetti.
    o Repeat this, only ask her to fill the container and pour out the pieces on your hands.

Real Life Reflections: "I'm another breastfeeding mom with a Daddy's girl.Cerridwen's favorite game is one, two, THREE! On one and two, we lift her slightly, and on three we raise her high above our heads (like the baby-toss game, except we don't let go). This game will pull her out of just about any sort of moody behavior, and she likes it best when Daddy does it, at least Yearly because he lifts her higher and doesn't get tired as quickly. (In my defense, I'm 5'1 and he's 6'8. She's a lot bigger percentage of my body weight than his!)

He also loves it when he runs around the yard with her, or when he takes her on a twilight walk before bedtime. These things all help her be calmer and happier. They also strengthen her relationship with her father and even, by showing me what a caring husband and father I married, strengthened the relationship between my husband and me.

Cerridwen is one and a half, and she loves it when we strip her down and sit her on the floor with washable markers. We put her on a non-stainable surface or on newspaper and give her poster board to draw on…but mostly, she draws on herself. She has lots of fun, and afterwards gets a bath. She likes the way the marker colors the water.She also like to play with pots, pans and spoons while we cook, she LOVES story time, and she really enjoys being danced around with music." – Monkey, AbsoluteWrite.com

Month nineteen:

"Most of us become parents long before we have stopped being children." -- Mignon McLaughlin, *The Second Neurotic's Notebook*, 1966

What to Expect:

- She'll probably put food on her utensil with her hands, and then lift it to her mouth.

- She's able to walk and talk steadier, but is still have trouble with pronunciation and coordination.

- Your daughter is probably going to start saying "NO" more often (it is the word she's heard most of her life, after all), so following through with positive direction about how this is unacceptable must remain consistent.

Developmental Tips:

- Help your daughter develop relaxation at night by singing her lullabies or reading her stories (or both!).

- Your daughter may still have difficulty sleeping through the night, so help her develop the ability to put herself back to sleep by keeping cuddling, reassurances, and soothing quick and putting her back to bed.

- Help your daughter get over fears of monsters and goblins under her bed or in her closet by being truthful and up front right from the beginning so she'll never doubt this and she'll be able to calm herself down.

Ideas For Activities:

- Continue coloring with your daughter.

- Continue reading to your daughter.

- Tracing to Develop Matching Skills:

    o Collect cookie cutters, keys, and jar covers.

    o Place each item on a piece of construction paper and trace them with a marker.

    o Place the paper in front of your daughter with each item on the matching tracing.

    o Take off one or two items at a time and ask her where she thinks they belong.

    o Remove more and more items until she's able to match everything without help.

Real Life Reflections: "I can't help watching the news and worrying that my daughter will be Year of it someday. What if she gets kidnapped? What if she gets lost? What if she's in an accident? I have to stop thinking like this, I know, or else I'll miss out on bonding with her. I don't want to lose out on her just because I worry too much." – Craig, Rhode Island

Month twenty:

"If you want children to keep their feet on the ground, put some responsibility on their shoulders." -- Abigail Van Buren

What to Expect:

- Don't be surprised if your daughter is awake and ready to start her day before the sun rises.

- Your daughter is going to resist naptime and want to eliminate it all together, but this is a huge mistake – children need time to recharge their batteries, calm their minds, and recoup.
- Molars are still going to give your daughter trouble for the next few months, so prepare to help with pain management.

Developmental Tips:

- Your daughter may be ready to develop toilet training techniques by now, so give it a try without putting unneeded pressure on her.
- Help develop your daughter's behavior by modeling it yourself – if you're grouchy and stubborn, she will act the same way. If you're positive and happy, she will mirror these behaviors.
- Help your daughter develop self-guidance by not being too permissive.

Ideas For Activities:

- Bring your daughter out to lunch to a kid-friendly restaurant like Chuck-E-Cheese as a "special occasion" place.

- Find reading groups at the library and bookstore to attend with your daughter.

- Make a Puzzle to Teach How to Use Them:

- Gather five or six old greeting cards and cut the front of each of them off.
- Using a 1-inch square hole puncher, punch out four squares from each card.
- Place the cards and corresponding pieces on the floor in front of your daughter.
- Show her how to fit the square pieces where they belong on one of the cards.
- Encourage her to do this with your help with the rest of the cards.
- Store the cards and their pieces in a resealing storage bag for future use.

Real Life Reflections: "I can't wait until she's big enough to play outside games with. I can't wait until I can push her down a slide, or play t-ball with her. I can't wait to teach her how to ride a bike. In the meantime, I can't wait until she's 100% potty trained." – Gene, California

Month twenty-one:

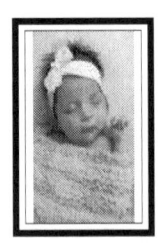

"The quickest way for a parent to get a child's attention is to sit down and look comfortable." -- Lane Olinghouse

What to Expect:

- She might start being rougher with her toys.
- Writing on walls could become an issue.
- Rejecting a high chair or booster seat might happen.

Developmental Tips:

- Help your daughter develop an early understanding of what is right and what is wrong by explaining why she is being disciplined.
- Help your daughter understand boundaries by being clear and consistent, and then following through.
- Help your daughter develop an early respect for her belongings by showing her how to gently put things away, rather than throwing them.

Ideas For Activities:

- Help your daughter understand sounds by using common household items at playtime.

- Give your daughter an old phone or a toy phone to have pretend conversations with her on.

- Develop Fine Mother Skills Using Oat Cereal:

    o Place oat cereal in front of your daughter in a small plastic bowl.

    o Next to the bowl, place a plastic jar with the lid loosened.

    o Ask her to fill the jar with the cereal.

    o She'll need to remove the lid, and then add the cereal one piece at a time.

    o When she finishes, ask her to dump it back into the bowl.

    o Encourage her to repeat this game until she grows tired of it and eats the cereal. ☺

Real Life Reflections: "When my twenty-one month old daughter started screaming every time it was time to get dressed, I finally started singing the put your clothes on song. To the tune of the hokey pokey, 'You put your head in, your put your arm in, you put the other arm in, and that you pull the shirt down, you do the put your close on dance and turn yourself around, that's what it's all about! Put your clothes on!' She loved it and she would do the little dance and laugh, I did the same with her pants, and she has never given me any trouble about getting dressed again!!" – Stacy Violette, from Newport News, VA.

Month twenty-two:

"Don't handicap your children by making their lives easy." -- Robert A. Heinlein

What to Expect:

- Your daughter might try pushing down gates that are blocking her from rooms or stairways she shouldn't access.

- She'll try harder to get into your things, even though she might fully understand that it's inappropriate.

- You will need to set lots of limits, or else you will be met with chaos and problems.

Developmental Tips:

- Help your daughter develop an early understanding that, if her toys are abused and broken, they will be thrown away and they will not be replaced.

- Introduce one or two new table manners techniques to help your daughter develop good mealtime manners.

- Remove things that could cause harm or hazards from your daughter's play area to help her develop a sense of safety and security.

Ideas For Activities:

- Draw pictures in sand or mud using a stick.

- Give your daughter an old computer keyboard and play with the buttons with her.

- Develop Coordination Using a Turkey Baster:

- o   Go outside, either on the ground or a picnic table, and place a plastic tablecloth down. Place two plastic bowls on the tablecloth.
- o   Fill one of the bowls with water and add a couple of drops of food coloring. Place the baster next to the bowls.
- o   Show your daughter how to use the baster, paying close attention to the colored water into the baster.
- o   Squeeze the water out and into the bowl.
- o   Encourage your daughter to do the same.

Real Life Reflections: "I like keeping my girl with me when I'm having breakfast in the morning. She has no idea what I'm doing or what I'm saying to her, but I don't care. Maybe if I start now, she'll want to keep having breakfast with me when she gets older. I hope so." – John, Massachusetts

Month twenty-three:

"It is a wise father that knows his own child." -- William Shakespeare

What to Expect:

- Your daughter is going to want everything she sees on TV, or everything that catches her eye in stores.

- She may start being sassy and talking back.

- Don't be surprised if she starts manipulating others (like her grandmother) to get her way about something she heard "no" about at home.

Developmental Tips:

- Help your daughter develop self-respect by teaching her that she is able, by doing your best to take care of her, and by showing her how to care for herself in some ways.

- Help your daughter develop respect for others by teaching her that it's never okay to hurt anyone, to use mean words, or to cause harm to others in any other way.

- Help your daughter develop respect for other people's property by teaching her to handle things the way she would handle her own property, and to always treat things nicely no matter where she is or whom she is with.

Ideas For Activities:

- Get some ice cubes out and some construction paper out and use the ice with your daughter to make pictures on the paper with.

- Create sidewalk chalk art in the driveway or at the playground.

- Totally Tubular! Over the course of several weeks, gather tubes. These can be tubes from toilet paper, paper towels, aluminum foil and so on. Once you have a wide variety gathered, you're ready to begin.

    o Set all of the tubes on the floor in front of your daughter.

    o Start trying to fit them inside each other, all the while encouraging your daughter to do the same.

    o Praise her for each of her accomplishments.
    o Try fitting a ball or small toys inside and show her how to do the same.

o When she grows tired of this activity, break out some crayons and stickers so she can decorate the tubes.

Real Life Reflections: "My little girl is my hero. She was born with problems with her heart, but she made it through. It's hard for me to talk about, but I do anyway. She showed me that, even though she doesn't know what life is yet, it's worth fighting for. That gave me an understanding about mortality that I never had before. She held on without knowing what she was holding on to. How did she do that? How could I not do that if I'm faced with something bad in my life? She taught me things that I doubt a book could ever teach me." – Andrew, Oregon

Month twenty-four:

"Too often we give children answers to remember rather than problems to solve." -- Roger Lewin

What to Expect:

- She might be speaking between twenty and thirty words correctly.

- You may see reactions from your daughter if there are problems exhibited in front of her between other family members.

- Don't be surprised if she expects things to go wrong when placed in new situations or environments.

Developmental Tips:

- Help your daughter develop an attachment to cups, rather than the bottle, by treating it as though it is the best thing on earth and something she simply can't pass up.
- Help your daughter understand what is acceptable behavior by staying consistent whenever she is exploring behaviors and seeing what she can get away with.

- Your daughter may throw a screaming temper tantrum when she doesn't get her way, so helping her develop a firm understanding that this behavior will not work is imperative – don't give in.

Ideas For Activities:

- Set out several different sized cups, and a picture of water outside with your daughter and let her try filling the cups up.

- Experiment with glitter glue projects to see if either you or your daughter can handle them okay.

- Bits of What-Not:
    - Collect catalogs, junk mail, colorful paper wrappers, stickers, wrapping paper scraps, pasta, beans, and yarn.
    - Set everything in front of your daughter with a large piece of paper and some white glue.
    - Supervise your daughter while she uses the glue.
    - Encourage her to make pictures, patterns, or nothing at all (a random collage of stuff).
    - Make one of your own to show her how to glue things down, select things from catalogs, and tear off interesting sections of the junk mail.

Real Life Reflections: "I have three daughters, aged four, two, and one. With all three, my husband has always been amazed at how early they show a marked preference to him over other people besides me. Almost as son as we get them home, they seem to recognize him and calm down faster for him than other not-mommies. One thing that surprised us both was that it's often easier for him to get them to sleep as babies. I think its because he's so warm-blooded, deep-voiced, and still. Or maybe just that he can't nurse them, so they're not distracted by thoughts of food with him." – Catherine P. Businelle, Oregon

Year Three:

She's a Busy Little Bee!

"Certain is it that there is no kind of affection so purely angelic as of a father to a daughter. In love to our wives there is desire; to our sons, ambition; but to our daughters there is something which there are no words to express." -- Joseph Addison

Crib Notes:

- Don't dismiss her expressions of anger or stress as "a girl thing," because boys do this, too.

- If she gravitates more toward "girlie" things than you're comfortable with, there are a ton of toys that look like they're developed for boys and they're girl colors.

- Even if you feel like you don't know how to play with her, get in there and try anyway! Nine times out of ten, she'll teach you in some little way.

Month twenty-five:

"A father is available to help his daughter balance both her love and her anger toward her mother, to moderate the inevitable emotional extremes in the intense mother-daughter equation. With Daddy's steadying influence daughters can learn to be comfortable with healthy anger, rather than feeling that they must be eternal good girls who must at all costs conceal it." – Victoria Secunda

What to Expect:

- She might start biting as a way to express her anger or stress over a situation.

- If your daughter's needs are met, she might start whining more often than usual.

- She may not be as cooperative as she was in previous months.

Developmental Tips:

- Help develop positive behaviors by constantly using positive reinforcement.

- Help your daughter develop an understanding that, when she misbehaves there will be a consequence, through use of a "time out" area.

- Help your daughter develop an understanding of how to play in a positive way by giving her plenty of opportunities to observe and interact with other children at play.

Ideas For Activities:

- Toss around a ball of yarn outside or in an area where it won't tangle on anything dangerous, and see how she can wind it back up again.

- Give your daughter a square box and ask her to make it into a cake using her toys with your help.

- Worm Painting:

    o Gather the following materials: multi-colored yarn, multi-colored tempera paint, small containers (one for each color of paint), light colored construction paper, small containers of water, paper towels, and smocks.

    o Pour some paint into each container and thin it down slightly with water.

    o Cut the yarn into 1-foot lengths, and dip them into the paint.

o Squiggle the paint-dipped yarn all over the construction paper.

> **Real Life Reflections:** "My daughters were both terrified of public toilets when they were both just out of diapers, especially the ones that flush automatically. (It *IS* startling!) I started carrying post-it notes in my purse and would tape one up over the sensor before they sat down and *viola*, no scary flush." – Wendy Pinkston Cebula

Month twenty-six:

"Children have more need of models than of critics." – Carolyn Coats, *Things Your Dad Always Told You But You Didn't Want to Hear*

What to Expect:

- She will like playing around other children, but may not interact with other children during playtime.

- If you have an only child, you may notice your daughter being selfish and having difficulty sharing.

- Getting your daughter to sleep will continue to be a challenge.

Developmental Tips:

- Encourage development of social play and interactions by balancing independent playtime with interaction with other children.
- Help your daughter develop sharing skills by giving her constant and consistent praise each time you see her doing this.

- Help develop and stimulate your daughter's imagination by giving her toys that are open-ended and can be played with in multiple ways.

Ideas For Activities:

- Act out your daughter's favorite cartoon episode, if she has one, with her.

- Let your daughter put bows, ribbons, and barrettes in your hair, while she's putting them into her doll's hair.

- Toothbrush Painting:
    - Gather the following materials: old toothbrushes, tempera paint, paint trays (or paper plates), craft sticks, multi-colored construction paper, white paper, small containers of water, paper towels, and smocks.
    - Do not thin the paint down after it has been poured out into the paint trays.
    - Dip the toothbrushes into the paint, and then create splatters with them by brushing them against the craft knife.
    - Splatter on white paper and colored paper to experiment with how different they come out.

Real Life Reflections: "I've noticed with my daughter (just getting out of her terrible twos), that the less time watching television, the fewer disciplinary problems we have with her. I'm not saying TV is bad, and she's allowed to watch it, but I limit it more now. She recovers from most of her angry moments quickly, save for the occasional, huge tantrum." – Elizabeth, New York

Month twenty-seven:

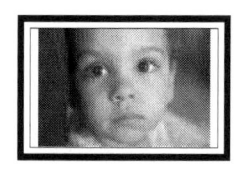

"Sing out loud in the car even, or especially, if it embarrasses your children." – Marilyn Penland

What to Expect:

- She may frustrate more easily, especially with things she's done over and over and it doesn't produce the results she's expecting.

- She'll probably enjoy rough and tumble play, but not as much as you would typically see from a brother or other boys that are peers.

- Stairs might still prove to be a bit tricky for your daughter to negotiate.

Developmental Tips:

- Help your daughter develop confidence in her abilities by showing her how to do things, but don't do them for her – stay close-by and let her do things on her own without help.

- Help your daughter develop her imagination through dramatic play where she makes up her own stories.

- Help develop your daughter's cognitive skills by playing sorting games, asking her to help sort laundry, or coordinating colors.

Ideas For Activities:

- Smear paint on to paper with your daughter using large pieces of paper, finger paints and craft sticks.

- Don't forget to continue taking lots of pictures of your daughter in action!

- Flower Garden:

    o Gather the following materials: white glue, green pipe cleaners, multi-colored felt squares, 8x10 (or larger) piece of green felt, scissors.

    o Cut flower shapes from the squares.

    o Cut bee shapes to match each flower.

    o Glue pipe cleaners to each flower head.

    o Place flowers in a line on the green felt.

- Ask daughter to match the colored bees with each colored flower.

> **Real Life Reflections:** "Even though I'm a new dad, I already feel worn out. If I dared to say that in front of my daughter's mother, I'm sure I'd have a swift kick in the rear. It's hard, though, because I wake up every time she makes a noise. Even if she makes a snoring type snort, I wake up thinking she needs something. I've never been a light sleeper, so it's hard to get use to this. My daughter's mom does the nighttime stuff because she's breast-feeding, so I won't tell her that I'm tired from being up at night. There's no reason for me to be up. I don't know what my problem is." – Alex, Australia

Month twenty-eight:

"The fundamental defect with fathers is that they want their children to be a credit to them. " – Bertrand Russell

What to Expect:

- Her balance and coordination will continue to improve.

- She'll enjoy new challenges and being praised for mastering (or trying) new things.

- She will love music – dancing, singing, or both.

Developmental Tips:

- Further develop your daughter's gross motor skills by thinking up games that involve her arms and legs.

- Further develop your daughter's fine motor skills by providing her with large sheets of paper and crayons so she can draw frequently.

- Encourage all developmental areas by playing with play-dough. It helps with fine motor skills, cognitive skills, and imagination just to name a few.

Ideas For Activities:

- Pretend to bake in a kitchen using cookie cutters and play-dough.

- Use cookie cutters to trace interesting shapes and patterns on paper.

- Mixing Colors in Plastic Bags:

    o Gather the following materials: shaving cream, food coloring, and zip-lock bags.

    o Place a ½ cup of shaving cream into each bag.

    o Ask your daughter to add a few drops of food coloring into each bag of shaving cream.

    o Seal the bags tightly.

    o Knead the bags with your daughter to mix the colors.

Real Life Reflections: "I'm lucky to have girls because I can protect them from guys like me. I know exactly what to look for. They're little now, but I still keep a watch out. If I lose that eagle-eyed perspective then I'm not doing my job. I feel bad for their future boyfriends because they don't stand a chance." – Christian, Mississippi

Month twenty-nine:

"Each day of our lives we make deposits in the memory banks of our children." – Charles R. Swindoll, *The Strong Family*

What to Expect:

- Your daughter may be ready to write or make simple shapes using crayons on large sheets of paper.

- She may want to spend a lot of time scribbling on paper while you read a story or give her instructions about an activity.

- She might show a lot more interest in helping in the kitchen.

Developmental Tips:

- Further develop fine motor skills by asking your daughter to trace over what you have created on paper, or by tracing in activity books.

- Further develop fine motor skills by teaching your daughter how to stay in the lines when coloring.

- Further develop fine motor skills by teaching your daughter how to clear a kitchen table after mealtime from beginning to end, allowing her to do as much as she possibly can on her own.

Ideas For Activities:

- Get some animal books from the library and look through them with your daughter.

- Teach your daughter about animal sounds using a video or improvising.

- Visit a Pet Shop or Zoo:

    o Gather the following materials: your daughter's favorite stuffed animal (or doll), disposable camera, and a small photo album.

    o Tell your daughter that you're bringing her to introduce he toy to some animals today.

    o Take pictures of each animal she's interested in.

    o Drop the film off at a 1-hour photo-mat and take your daughter to lunch.

o   Create a "what's this" photo album to look through with her.

Real Life Reflections: "We've never been the kind of family that eats at the table in the kitchen during meals. I like watching TV, so I never thought twice about us all eating in the living room. We read a lot of stories to my daughter (well, my wife does), and she asked us one day why we can't eat at the table like the bears in her story. We tried it and it's been our way of doing things from then on. She's said a lot about how she likes eating at the table like a family instead of watching TV. Reading has had a more positive influence on my daughter than just teaching her about words. I didn't expect that to happen at this age." – Geoff, Washington

Month thirty:

"Daughters are angles sent from above to fill our heart with unending love." – J. Lee

What to Expect:

- Your daughter might show preference for sweet foods, like fruits, over anything else and show a lot of resistance to eating greens.
- She might start demanding more "TV time" in comparison to previous months.
- She might have a hard time understanding why TV shows can't be watched over again like her videos or DVDs.

Developmental Tips:

- Help develop fine motor skills by giving your daughter lots of containers to put her toys away in.
- Help develop fine motor skills by giving your daughter a variety of puzzles to work with ranging from very easy to very challenging.
- Help develop cognitive thinking skills by giving your daughter mazes to attempt do on her own or with help.

Ideas For Activities:

- Blow bubbles in milk and show her what happens.
- Start teaching her basic games like Connect 4 and Candyland.
- Food Creatures:
  o Gather the following materials: paper plates, carrot sticks, pretzel sticks, celery sticks, raisins, halved grapes, nuts.
  o Place all the ingredients in the middle of the table in separate plates or a platter.
  o Make food creatures during snack time.

Real Life Reflections: "My middle son weaned (from nursing) at thirteen months on his own with no trouble. He never really looked back. My DD just weaned, at thirty months, about four weeks ago. She still asks for it sometimes. The first time she cried and cried like I'd broken her heart. It felt so bad. Now she takes the offered chocolate milk instead without much resistance. But she still misses it. Another thing that happened when my son weaned was that he really didn't want to cuddle with me as much as he did before. My daughter still loves to cuddle despite losing her nursing." – Kristy26, AbosulteWrite.com forums

Month thirty-one

"How pleasant it is for a father to sit at his child's board. It is like an aged man reclining under the shadow of an oak which he has planted." – Walter Scott

What to Expect:

- Your daughter may want to start asserting independence by dressing herself.

- She may start arguing with you about what she's wearing.

- Expect resistance when it comes to brushing or combing her hair.

Developmental Tips:

- Further develop your daughter's fine motor skills by letting her button herself up and do her own zippers.
- Further develop fine motor skills and cognitive thinking skills by teaching your daughter how to tie her shoes.
- Further develop cognitive thinking skills by having as many conversations with your daughter as possible as often as possible.

Ideas For Activities:

- Start looking at preschools with your daughter and asking for some time to see how your daughter will play with the group.
- When reading to your daughter, ask her to mimic the sounds of animals or the voices she might think the people would make.
- Make Play Dough:
    o Gather the following materials: 1 ½ cups of flour, 1 cup of salt, 3 tbsp. of oil, powdered drink mix, 1 cup of boiling water.
    o Combine the first four ingredients, and mix thoroughly.

- Add the fifth ingredient, knead dough until smooth.

> **Real Life Reflections:** "I think I read every development and milestone book on the market, eagerly hoping my daughter would reach these moments on time. She never ever did what the books said. They said she'd walk before she was one, and she didn't. They said she'd sleep through the night after a few months, and she still doesn't. They said a bunch of other stuff that was just a bunch of bunk. I let it be, though, after my daughter's pediatrician told me to stop obsessing and just let her grow. I hated hearing that I was obsessing, but he was right. I let it go and, when I did, I started enjoying my daughter a lot more. There were no hang-up's, just fun." – Phillip, Maine

Month thirty-two

"The greatest gift I ever had Came from God, and I call him Dad! " – Anonymous

What to Expect:

- You may see less accidents when potty training.

- Your daughter might show interest in watching birds, butterflies, and small animals in nature.

- She might show interest in learning her ABC's and 123's.

Developmental Tips:

- Further develop cognitive thinking skills by asking your daughter a lot of questions that require more than a yes or no answer.

- Further develop cognitive thinking skills by giving your daughter choices and encouraging problem solving whenever appropriate.

- Further develop cognitive thinking skills by teaching your daughter new things that will enable her to better learn how to listen and follow directions.

Ideas For Activities:

- Make a fruit salad together, and serve it over yogurt.
- Teach your daughter games like patty-cake.
- Make Play Dough Creatures:
    - Gather the following materials: homemade play dough, feathers, buttons, large beads, pipe cleaners, craft sticks, and clothespins.
    - Divide the play dough between you and your daughter.
    - Place materials into separate containers.
    - Create creatures.

Real Life Reflections: "My daughter already loves to cook. I thank my mom for that because she's here everyday while my wife and I work to help take care of her. They make the family's dinner together and sometimes they make dessert, too. My mom isn't the type that will let her stand by and watch. She does it all with her, except what will burn or cut her. It's pretty cool to say my little girl had dinner waiting for me on the table when I got home. No one believes how little she is when they find out she's only two." – Colin, Maine

Month thirty-three

"You will always be your child's favorite toy." –Vicki Lansky, *Trouble-Free Travel with Children*, 1991

What to Expect:

- She'll be better at running and will do so quite often.

- She might be able to ride a bike with training wheels.
- She'll be able to climb better with less falling and clumsiness.

Developmental Tips:

- Further develop cognitive thinking skills by teaching your daughter about colors.
- Further develop cognitive thinking skills by giving your daughter activity books and problem solving toys to try attempting without help.
- Help your daughter develop her memory through games, like Memory, and by doing multi-step tasks.

Ideas For Activities:

- Fruit of Vegetable Picking! Depending on the time of year, you could pick:

    o Apples

    o Pumpkins

    o Garden vegetables

    o Berries

- ✓ Use this as an opportunity to discuss quantities, shapes, sizes, colors, textures, and of course taste.
- Make shapes out of pieces of bread by squishing them.
- Make masks out of paper plates and then use them to play with.

Real Life Reflections: "My favorite childhood memory with my dad is very very early – I remember being very young (probably under age three) and in one of those baby seats that attach to adult bikes. I remember riding through this park on the back of dad's bike, we were going fast, it was a cool spring day, and the sun was shining through the leaves above us. I remember feeling so exhilarated from the speed, yet safe – I knew my Dad was keeping me safe." – Erin Partridge, New York

Month thirty-four

"The joys of parents are secret, and so are their griefs and fears." – Francis Bacon, Sr

What to Expect:

- She might be able to name up to five of her body Years without help.

- Her vocabulary might be between thirty and fifty words by now.

- She might be able to understand the differences between soft and hard, warm and cold, bright and dark, and so on.

Developmental Tips:

- Help your daughter develop cognitive thinking skills by teaching her about shapes.

- Help your daughter develop cognitive thinking skills be teaching her about numbers, starting with number one (there's one apple left in the basket, can you pick out one toy, do you have one nose, and so on).

- Help your daughter develop early math skills be asking her how many French fries are left on her plate, talking about objects of different sizes, and giving her indications of how much time is left before bedtime.

Ideas For Activities:

- Teach your daughter how to play 'Go Fish," and "Old Maid."
- Go to the park and fly some paper airplanes.
- Paper Towel Dying:
    o Gathering the following materials: paper towels, waxed paper, food coloring, plastic containers (one for each color), and water.
    o Mix food coloring and water in each container. Your daughter may want to help with this step.
    o Lay paper towels into the containers. You can add the paper towel to more than one color to create an interesting mix.
    o Let the paper towel dry completely on the waxed paper.
    o Use stencils or cookie cutters to trace and cut out shapes for more craft projects in the future.

Real Life Reflections: "My family enjoys expressing gratitude for just about everything every change we get. So, whenever my girl gets a gift she likes to make thank you cards. My wife got her into this habit and it's been great. I like passing them out instead of mailing them because I like hearing everyone say what a good job she's done on the cards. I bring her along sometimes so she can hear that praise. It really encourages her to do it more and it really builds her confidence." – Brad, Vermont

Month thirty-five

"If your children spend most of their time in other people's houses, you're lucky; if they all congregate at your house, you're blessed." – Mignon McLaughlin, *The Second Neurotic's Notebook*, 1966

What to Expect:

- She could be speaking in longer sentences more clearly by now.

- You might see her ability to copy shapes, such as circles, increase.

- She'll be able to say her first and last name when asked.

Developmental Tips:

- Help your daughter develop organizational skills by giving her several objects and asking her to sort them with like objects in the grouping.
- Further develop cognitive thinking skills, as well as fine motor skills through playing board games.

- Playing games like "Twister" or other games where motion is involved with help your daughter further develop gross motor skills.

Ideas For Activities:

- Start using an Easy Bake oven with your daughter with a lot of your help.

- Spread some glue on to Popsicle sticks and sprinkle them with glitter.

- Milk Jug Drop:

- Gather the following materials: find an empty ½ gallon milk jug, and clothespins.
- Place all the clothespins inside the jug and place the cap loosely into place.
- Ask your daughter to remove the cap and dump out all the clothespins.
- Ask your daughter to put them all back in one by one.

Real Life Reflections: "My youngest, now three, loves to sit down with paper and glue and do a 'craft.' I keep little pieces of foam and confetti-type stuff around, and she has a ball creating patterns. (Or not-so-patterns.) For that matter, my five year old love the same.

Both girls like whatever their daddy does with them that's physical. In other words, he'll hold them up off the ground and swing them back and forth, or give them piggyback rides. And he loves to teach them about nature and animals. Museums and parks and those things are great." – Janna, AbsoluteWrite.com forums

Month thirty-six

"A father is always making his baby into a little woman. And when she is a woman he turns her back again. " –
Enid Bagnold

What to Expect:

- She might be able to classify some or all of the primary colors.
- She could be playing "make believe" more often.
- Use of pronouns such as "I," "we," and "you" might happen more often.

Developmental Tips:

- Further develop fine motor skills and cognitive thinking skills by giving your daughter a lot of problem solving games and continue to give her puzzles.
- Help your daughter further develop cognitive thinking skills by playing games where she has

to figure out what is the same and what is different.

- Go to the library and find age appropriate books containing science experiments to further develop her fine motor skills and cognitive thinking skills through scientific experimentations.

Ideas For Activities: Active Reading Time

- Be sure to set aside at least fifteen minutes to a half and hour depending on your work schedule per day, if possible.

- Ask your daughter to pick out several books, but keep in mind that just because she picks out ten books that doesn't necessarily mean she wants to read all of them. She might just like the cover.

- Ask her to pick a book, and then ask her why she made that choice. Let her chatter, answer any questions she has, and let her changer her mind about her selection if she desires.

- Start reading the story, allowing her to interrupt with questions and thoughts. This means she's interested and engaged.

- If you finish the story, ask her what it is she liked best about the book. If you don't finish the story, ask her if she'd like to set the book aside in a special palce for your next time together.

Real Life Reflections: "Both our girls are fascinated by Daddy's facial hair. They like to play with it when he doesn't shave.

He grows a beard occasionally. When Faerie was, oh, a year and a half or so, he'd hold her on his lap and she'd scratch her fingernails over the beard and giggle like crazy. She was disappointed when he shaved it, but he re-grew it six months later or so and she didn't like it much. When he shaved it last time she grinned and said, 'Now I can see your cheeks!' Sometimes they ask him to re-grow it again; sometimes he asks them if he should and they say no. But they find the whole process really interesting, so that might be something fun for Dads to try when the girls are a little past infancy"
– December Quinn

Year Four:

The Challenges Continue, and There Will be More!

"A daughter may outgrow your lap, but she will never outgrow your heart." – Author Unknown

Month thirty-seven

"A daughter is a little girl who grows up to be a friend." –
Author Unknown

What to Expect:

- Expect your daughter to express more frustrations when things don't go the way they're supposed to (in her mind, or in reality).

- She can probably distinguish between good and bad, and be able to express this knowledge clearly.

- She might be able to express herself with more words than before.

Developmental Tips:

- Help your daughter develop language skills by avoiding baby talk, and speak to her the way you would speak to her mother or other peers.

- Further develop cognitive thinking and memory skills by asking your daughter to write or draw something you name. For example, name a circle and ask her to draw that shape.
- Help your daughter develop body language by using a lot of it yourself.

Ideas For Activities:

- Cover empty food boxes with construction paper, and then draw on windows and doors to create a mini-city to play with your daughter with.
- Glue googley eyes and paper feet on to pom-poms to create imaginary creatures to play with.
- Have a Puppet Show:
    o Get out a pair of her socks and a pair of your socks.
    o Draw some silly faces on them using washable markers.
    o Put your socks on your hands and encourage your daughter to do the same.
    o Use silly voice sand dramatic gestures to get her interested and involved in this activity.
    o Let your daughter guide you through the dialogue in order to encourage expression of

feelings, asking questions, and stimulation of her imagination.

Real Life Reflections: "My three-year old insists she's going to marry Daddy when she grows up. Daddy just smiles and says he loves her or that's she's wonderful; we know in a few years he'll have to explain to her that he can't marry her, but for not he enjoys it.

Also, he reads her bedtime story-- they like it better when he does it and it's special Daddy-only moment he has with the kids. When he's finished with the story and kissed them goodnight, he turns off the lights, stands in the doorway and says, 'Okay, now. Hunker down; close your eyes, no talking, go to sleep, and sweet dreams! (Sometimes he adds, 'And everybody stay in your own beds.' But usually they ask to sleep together and we let them.) I love you and see you in the morning.'

The LOVE it. They follow his directions exactly, giggling the whole time. a few times he's been away for whatever reason and I've out the to bed and they didn't like that I didn't give the speech, but if I do they say I'm not saying it right." – Stacia Kane, Southwest England

Month thirty-eight

"The most important thing a father can do for his children is to love their mother." – Henry Ward Beecher

What to Expect:

- She should be able to eat without trouble using a spoon.

- You may notice her using more eye contact when speaking to people, or when being spoken to by others.

- She may prefer to squat, rather then bending over, to pick things up.

Developmental Tips:

- Further develop your daughter's language skills by reading to her as often as possible – this is one the best ways to give her a wide variety of words, vocal incantations, and enunciations.

- Help your daughter understand what "potty mouth" is by correcting use of bad words promptly and by not using them around her, which will further develop her language skills.

- Encourage language development through use of rhyming games.

Ideas For Activities:

- Sing silly songs and nursery rhymes with your daughter.

- Spread glue on to construction paper with your daughter, and then encourage her to glue different shaped pasta all over the place.

- Football Game Interruption:

    o The next time you're watching a football game (or any other show you routinely watch), lie on the floor.

    o Before you know it, your daughter will either be tripping over you or jumping on you – let he interrupt the show.

    o Take this opportunity for tickle time and other "indoor appropriate" (have to keep Mom from biting her nails . . . or snapping) rough housing!

    o Don't go too far so she doesn't get hurt or grow too exhausted – and be sure to set some gentle rules about no punching, biting, pulling hair, or kicking. Have fun!

Real Life Reflections: "One thing he always says, that always gets to me, "I'm the first man they will ever love. So, I have to be the type of guy I want them to love." He also thinks its important to teach them how to stand up to boys, so they don't get pushed around. He never wants boys talking his girls into things they don't want to do." – Megan, Australia

Month thirty-nine

"If you want your children to improve, let them overhear the nice things you say about them to others." – Haim Ginott

What to Expect:

- She should be able to name many familiar objects without help.

Raising Your Daughter from Ages 0-10   115

- She will be making big strides in stacking and sorting.

- She should be able to jump with two feet.

Developmental Tips:

- Help your daughter with healthy eating habits by offering several smaller meals, rather than the typical three meals and two snack routine.

- Help develop fine motor skills by playing traditional finger and toes games, like "This Little Piggy Went to Market," and "The Itsy-Bitsy Spider."

- Help develop fine and gross motor skills by playing games like "The Wheels on the Bus," and "I'm a Little Tea Pot."

Ideas For Activities:

- Cut shapes from potatoes and ask your daughter to dip them into paint and stamp on to paper with them.

- Have a tickle fight!

- Make a Squiggle, Get a Giggle!
    - Set out markers, crayons, and a large piece of paper.

- o Start squiggling all over the paper with a crayon in one hand and a marker in the other. Encourage your daughter to do the same.

- o Neither of you will be able to resist all the giggling!

- o When all the paper and colors have been used up, ask your daughter if she can see any common shapes or animals.

> **Real Life Reflections:** "When my sister was in preschool, they had this song for learning the numbers 1-10: One one one you're so much fun fun fun, Two two two I sure like you, and so on. And the line for eight was, Eight eight eight you're really great great great! She changed it to – eight eight eight I'm on a date with Dad! That song sure got a lot of mileage." – Danger Jane, AbsoluteWrite.com forums

Month forty

"We never know the love of our parents for us till we have become parents." – Henry Ward Beecher

What to Expect:

- You may see an increase in temper tantrums.

- She might start expressing irrational thoughts and beliefs.

- She could be throwing a ball and riding a tricycle like a pro by now.

Developmental Tips:

- Help your daughter develop an understanding that temper tantrums will not get her way, and work on ways to prevent temper tantrums before they happen.

- Further develop your daughter's reading skills by reading to her often, as well as keeping books around her in as many rooms as possible (on shelves, in baskets, under end tables, and other easily accessible areas of the room).

- Further develop memory skills by asking your daughter about books you read in previous days, as well as by asking her what her favorite book is and why.

Ideas For Activities:

- Teach your daughter the basics of playing Frisbee.

- Try teaching simple pen and paper games like tic tac toe.

- Go For a Bike Ride:

  o Even if you're walking alongside your daughter as she peddles along, or if she's riding in a child seat on your bike, take this opportunity to interact.

  o Talk about what you see and ask her what she's looking at. Encourage questions by asking some of your own.

  o After the ride, ask her what her favorite Year was and then share what you liked the best.

Real Life Reflections: "My three-year-old tells everyone her boyfriend is Diego (from Go! Diego

Go!), but she carries around a baby doll and tells people I'm the father. She's also obsessed with kangaroos." – Matt Dinniman, Tuscon, AZ

Month forty-one

"Mother Nature is wonderful. Children get too old for piggy-back rides just about the same time they get too heavy for them." – Author Unknown

What to Expect:

- Don't be surprised if your daughter asks you to set a place at the dinner table for her imaginary friend.

- Your daughter may experience challenges with bed-wetting.

- You should be able to understand about 75% of what your daughter is saying to you now.

Developmental Tips:

- Further improve fine motor skills by teaching your daughter how to use safety scissors.
- Help your daughter develop counting skills be teaching her to use her fingers to keep track.
- Further develop manners by teaching your daughter how to behave at birthday parties and other outings.

Ideas For Activities:

- Have a pillow fight!
- Try cutting out snowflakes.
- Car Games:
    - The next time you're riding in your car with your daughter, pass the time with a car game – literally.
    - Make a funny noise for each color car you pass, assigning a different sound for each different color.
    - Before you know it, your little person will be laughing and copying all your funny noises – while learning her colors better.

- Ask her to make up her own noises when you pass or see other things like busses, big rigs, and taxi cabs.

Real Life Reflections: "My three year old has what we call 'Fear of Organizational Seating.' For instance, you can take here into a crowd and she's fine, but put her in a movie theater (or a Shamu show at Sea World) and she's no good. Even at "It's a Small World" at Disney World, she had big issues. But once out and among the throngs of people, fine." – Jason, Georgia

Month forty-two

"Our daughters are the most precious of our treasures, the dearest possessions of our homes and the objects of our most watchful love." – Margaret E. Sangster

What to Expect:

- When asked who her friends are, you daughter may recite the names of everyone she knows – including friends of yours she's only met a couple of times.

- Don't be surprised if you see your daughter replaying stressful situations or experiences that bothered her using her stuffed animals or dolls.

- She probably can identify most colors by sight by now.

Developmental Tips:

- Help your daughter develop an understanding of the world surrounding her by taking her for walks and explaining to her what is in your neighborhood (this will increase her vocabulary, as well).

- Further develop your daughter's language skills by teaching her new songs and poems on a regular basis (books from the library will help with this).

- Further develop listening skills by buying books that have tapes accompanying them, and following along as the tape plays.

Ideas For Activities:

- Show your daughter how to make fizzy water using Alka-Seltzer.
- Teach her how to make funny hairstyles using shampoo.
- Time for "T"
  - Go out and purchase a standard pre-school or t-ball set, as well as a selection of baseball-sized colored soft balls.
  - Set the game up outside or in your basement with your daughter, all the while explaining the basics of the game.
  - Let her select what kind of ball she'd like to hit, as well as which ball you'll hit on your turn.
  - Ask her what she liked about the game, which ball she like the best, and if she has ideas for other games.

Real Life Reflections: "I don't want my daughter to think I'm too tired to spend time with her, so I never tell her I'm tired after a long or bad day at work. My family tells me I'm making a mistake, but I figure she's going to go through enough rejection later on. Why does she need to with her dad, too?" – Bryant, New Jersey

Month forty-three

"The guys who fear becoming fathers don't understand that fathering is not something perfect men do, but something that perfects the man. The end product of child raising is not the child but the parent." –Frank Pittman, *Man Enough*

What to Expect:

- You'll probably see more interaction during social playtime in comparison to previous months.

- Your daughter may prefer playing "domestic" games, rather than games that are more adventurous.

- She may weigh up to 30 pounds and be up to 3 feet tall.

Developmental Tips:

- Help your daughter develop new and less limited playtime rituals by offering a wide variety of toys, rather than only exposing her to gender specific toys.

- Help your daughter develop a sense of seeing things from other's points of view in order to encourage better sharing. For example, explain to her how she would feel if her friend didn't share with her and then tell her that's how her friend feels when she behaves this way.

- Help your daughter develop an understanding of rules, order, and limitations by encouraging her to play games with friends often. This will also help her develop skills with patience.

Ideas For Activities:

- Experiment with your daughter about what will sink in the tub and what won't.

- Take turns trying to pick up small objects dropped into the tub using tongs.

- Finger Painting Fun:

- You'll need an assortment of supplies for this activity:

  ✓ Assorted finger paints

  ✓ Smock
  ✓ Large pieces of paper

  ✓ Large paintbrushes

  ✓ Containers of water

  ✓ Sponge stampers

- Set up the painting area outside, if possible, or in an area of the home where your daughter can make a mess.

- Make sure she's wearing her smock, and encourage her to use her hands more than anything else.

- Get your hands in there and show her what kinds of swirls and patterns you can make.

- Use the paintbrushes and sponge stampers to make patterns, textures, and pictures in the paint before it dries.

Real Life Reflections: "I had no idea what I'd do when my girl was born because I'm not in touch with my feminine side at all. Nothing girly about me at all. I thought my girlfriend would spend the most time with her while I just watched. I was wrong. She's easier to take care of then I thought. Except for the diapers year. I left that up to her mother back then." – Todd, Nebraska

Month forty-four

"He opened the jar of pickles when no one else could. He was the only one in the house who wasn't afraid to into the basement by himself. He cut himself shaving, but no one kissed it or got excited about it. It was understood when it rained, he got the car and brought it around to the door. When anyone was sick, he went out to get the prescription filled. He took lots of pictures ... but he was never in them." – Erma Bombeck

What to Expect:

- Conflicts over toys will continue.

- She will express an understanding between boys and girls.

- She might become a more active participant in morning routines and rituals.

Developmental Tips:

- Help your daughter further develop language and vocabulary skills by keeping magnetized letters on the refrigerator (or any other surface at her eye level) and encourage her to try spelling.

- Further develop your daughter's sense of self-worth by constantly reaffirming how valuable she is to the family, as well as how much you love her.

- Further develop your daughter's sense of self and self-worth by explaining to her what is hers and allowing her to claim ownership to her belongings.

Ideas For Activities:

- Take turns trying to toss milk bottle caps into a bowl.

- Make some beanbags and ask your daughter to come up with ways to play with them.

- Build a Fort!

    o Gather several lightweight blankets, sheets, and beach towels.

- Bring your kitchen chairs, as well as any stools you might have, into your living room.

- Once you have put all the large blankets and sheets on to form the basic structure of the fort, ask your daughter to help by adding the towels.

- Ask your daughter to decorate the inside of the fort with some toys, books, stuffed animals, and anything else she might want to play with inside with you.

- Let her imagination guide this activity, but don't be too afraid to offer some suggestions of your own as the ideas hit you.

- If the fort is out of the way, consider leaving it up for a couple of days for extended playtime.

Real Life Reflections: "Baby talk drives me nuts with other kids, but I kind of think it's cute when my daughter does it with me. It mostly happens when we're playing. She has an assertive voice when she wants her way, so it's kind of backwards. I guess she's an individual and not a 'typical' girl." – Patrick, UK

Month forty-five

"He who is taught to live upon little owes more to his father's wisdom than he who has a great deal left him does to his father's care." – William Penn

What to Expect:

- She might still have sensitivity to strong smells and strong flavors.

- Don't be surprised if naptime is now a thing of the past, no matter how cranky and tired your daughter is in the afternoon.

- She's going to try negotiating bedtime, so stay consistent and tell her it is not negotiable.

Developmental Tips:

- Help develop and nurture your daughter's need to please by allowing her to help with household chores.

- Further develop your daughter's ability to make decisions and figure out her tastes by letting her pick out her outfits the night before (this will also give her more time if the morning routine is short).

- Help your daughter further develop her self-esteem by constantly praising her actions, as well as talking to her about how proud you are of her.

Ideas For Activities:

- Transform your daughter's room temporarily into an office or classroom for more elaborate playtime.

- Make towers out of toys that aren't stacking toys or blocks to see how high it can be built before it falls over.

- Visit a Fire Station!

    o Try planning a trip to the fire station well in advance to best utilize the time, as well as get permission to be in the station.

    o See if someone is available for a brief tour, explain how a fire station operates, and so your daughter might be able to get on to one of the trucks.

- Purchase a coloring book and a reading book to explore this experience further once you return home.

- Don't forget to take along a camera, lots of film, and take lots of pictures of everything. Gather brochures, pamphlets, and other flat paper items to make a scrapbook later with your daughter.

> **Real Life Reflections:** "My middle daughter was very unlike her two sisters, which is weird because the youngest and the oldest are very much alike. It's almost like she doesn't belong to this family sometimes, which makes for a very interesting home life." – Richard, Texas

Month forty-six

"I have always looked at life as a voyage, mostly wonderful, sometimes frightening. In my family and

friends I have discovered treasure more valuable than gold." – Jimmy Buffet

What to Expect:

- She should be able to brush her teeth with supervision.

- She may be showing some hesitation when it comes to trying new foods.

- She's probably ready to leave the home and be cared for in a daycare setting, or in someone else's home.

Developmental Tips:

- Help develop your daughter's creativity by allowing her to make things her way, rather than the way you perceive how things should be made.

- Further develop imaginary skills through dress up.

- Help your daughter further develop her confidence in the kitchen by allowing her to decorate cupcakes, garnishing cereals with fruits, making sandwiches using several ingredients, and adding toppings to homemade pizzas.

Ideas For Activities:

- Pretend one of her stuffed animals is alive and going through the day with the two of you.

- Ask your daughter to pick out a book, and then tell a story based upon what is on the book's cover.

- Play With Clay or Play Dough:

  o Set out many colors of clay or play dough on your kitchen table or any other wipe able surface.

  o Set out cookie cutters, plastic utensils, and small rolling pins.

  o Start making imaginative shapes, using the supplies on the table, and making creatures while encouraging your daughter to do the same.

  o All her to mix colors, and see what she discovers.

  o Play with whatever you make and encourage her to do the same. Let her imagination guide this activity.

Real Life Reflections: "She's constantly following me around with piles of books, but she doesn't want me to read them all. I'd get frustrated and tell her to put the books back unless she wanted me to read them. Then, I realized she picked what she liked and changed her mind by the time she got to me. Like her mother says, she's a [young] woman and she has the right to change her mind. I think I'm in trouble." – Mitch, Queens

Month forty-seven

"Mother Nature, in her infinite wisdom, has instilled within each of us a powerful biological instinct to reproduce; this is her way of assuring that the human race, come what may, will never have any disposable income." – Dave Barry

What to Expect:

- She might be able to do an under-hand throw with a ball.

- You might notice that she's able to point out what some words say when you're reading to her.

- She should be able to hold utensils, pencils, and crayons better.

Developmental Tips:

- Further develop good habits with hygiene by asking your daughter to wash her hands before dinner, as well as after each time she uses the bathroom.
- Use your daughter's name as much as possible, rather than a pet name, when speaking to her in order to further develop her sense of self.

- Help your daughter develop a sense of trust when you tell her you're proud of her by showing her – display her artwork, display pictures of her engaged in activities, and display pieces of her writing all around the house.

Ideas For Activities:

- Ask your daughter to draw a picture of a dream she remembers.

- Pretend a blanket is a magic carpet and see what your daughter's imagination does during this game!

- Be a Volunteer:
    - Ask your daughter's teacher if you can volunteer in her classroom.
    - Volunteer to read a story during your daughter's weekly library time.
    - Chaperone during field trips and other class outings.
    - Offer to teach a craft, or other activity during class time.
    - Bring some of these experiences home with you and your daughter to play school with her.

Real Life Reflections: "My wife hung up what looks like preschool classroom pictures all over the house. We have crayons with the colors written on them in the living room, pictures of shoes with words written in them in the mudroom, pictures of food with words on them in the kitchen, and stuff like that. It's weird to me because my mother never did stuff like that, but

> my daughter seems to really love it." – Nicholas, Pennsylvania

Month forty-eight

"The most extraordinary thing in the world is an ordinary man and an ordinary woman and their ordinary children." – G. K. Chesterton

What to Expect:

- Your daughter will be more independent, and will want to take care of herself more often.

- She will be expressing herself more, and discussing what she likes and dislikes more often.

- Refinement of gross motor skills will begin and continue throughout the year.

Developmental Tips:

- Help your daughter develop an idea of time and structure through use of daily routines.
- Practice snapping and buttoning with your daughter to further develop this skill and prevent frustrations.
- Further develop word recognition by posting "sight words" throughout your home by labeling common items or hanging post-it notes on windows at her eye level.

Ideas For Activities:

- Ask your daughter to pick out several books, talk about what her favorite Years of each book are, and then write a story of her own (with your help) using only her favorite Years from the books.
- Make up stories about what her toys are doing after she goes to sleep.
- Bring Your Daughter to Work:
    - If your job is appropriate (in other words, safe for children), plan in advance so your employer can give you proper permissions, and your co-workers will know what's going on.
    - Dress your daughter up fancy (she'll show you what she wants to wear), allowing her to

pick our some jewelry and other fancy things (hats, scarves, purses, etc.).
- Either pack a lunch with yours, or plan to take her out to where you usually take your lunch break.
- Involve her in as much of your job as you can. If you think she might get bored, plan ahead by packing a pretend briefcase with coloring books, crayons, paper, books, crayons, and pencils.

Real Life Reflections: "When my daughter, Molly, was four, I had a pivotal lesson in punishment. For whatever reason I can longer remember, I sent her to her room. She stomped up the stairs and slammed the door. That was fine. I didn't expect her to be happy about it. Fortunately I remained in the kitchen near a large picture window. Out of the corner of my eye, I saw movement and looked just in time to se Molly running off. She had climbed out her window onto the roof of the porch, shimmied down the post, and was running off. I finally found her hiding under a large bush beyond the barn.

Many parents would have punished her for running off, but I took her behavior to mean that if I punished her, she would feel wronged and would pay me back – as hard as she could. That's who she was. I had

Raising Your Daughter from Ages 0-10   141

to find a better way. She has never been punished since. It took me four years to learn the lesson, but when I looked at her behavior as my clue to what she needed instead of an indictment, our relationship changed. I've never regretted letting go of punishment." – Bonnie Harris, author of *Confident Parents, Remarkable Kids: 8 Principles for Raising Kids You'll Love to Live With* (Adams Media, Sept. 2008)

Year Five:

You're Doing Great, and You're Still Alive!

"A daughter is a little girl who grows up to be a friend." –
Author Unknown

Crib Notes:

- The fact that you may not be ready to send your daughter to preschool or daycare yet is not a clear indication that she is not ready to go. Don't be afraid, she'll be fine!
- Don't be surprised if your little girl wants you to pretend you're the "mommy" or the "wife" when you're playing with dolls with her.
- Try not to push her toward doing only activities that you prefer or feel like doing – let her guide playtime as much as possible.

Month forty-nine

"A daughter is a gift of love." -- Author Unknown

What to Expect:

- You might notice your daughter using her tricycle less, and want to use her two-wheeler with training wheels more.

- She'll want to learn to play games that involve more than a few simple steps and be challenged more.

- She'll probably start drawing and forming letters or numbers in greater detail.

Developmental Tips:

- Sing the alphabet to your daughter as you write capital and lower case letters on paper for her and encourage her to copy you when you're finished.
- Help your daughter develop counting skills and math skills by numbering cut-out shapes on a piece of paper, removing some of the shapes,

and then adding them back all the while asking her how many are there.

- Sing lullabies and nursery rhymes to your daughter daily (if possible) to help her develop memorization skills.

Ideas For Activities:

- Draw or paint on scrap pieces of wood.

- Make a car out of an empty milk jug.

- Lock and Latch Board: (Make this ahead of time.)

    o You'll need the following materials to complete this project: 2 foot piece of shelving board; various locks, latches, and switches; felt; and a staple gun.

    o Fill one side of the board with locks, latches, and switches.

    o Wrap the back of the board, as well as the edges, with felt and staple it into place.

    o Sit on the floor with your daughter so the board sits in front of you, or on your lap, and play.

Real Life Reflections: "I have a daughter, now age 5.

My hubby made fun of me for saying that the baby could hear him in utero. Literally made fun of me. I make him talk to her, play guitar, etc. He thought it was a waste of time. Until...The birth went badly, we had an emergency c-section, and I was out cold for hours. The baby wouldn't stop screaming, so my husband tentatively said her name. She stopped screaming instantly. Every time he talked to her, she quieted and watched him. He was the only one that could keep her calm.

He talked to my belly lots with the second baby. And now he tells everyone that dads make a huge difference!" – heyjude, Absolutewrite.com forums

Month fifty

"The family is the test of freedom; because the family is the only thing that the free man makes for himself and by himself." -- Gilbert Keith Chesterton

What to Expect:

- She'll probably be writing her letters and numbers better.

- She may start talking about what she wants to do when she grows up.

- She may start reading along with you in familiar and favorite books.

Developmental Tips:

- Help your daughter further develop letter and number writing skills by showing her how to incorporate them into pictures she draws.
- Provide your daughter with coloring books and picture books about what she wants to do when she grows up in order to further develop the idea and dream making process.

- Help your daughter develop better reading skills by writing sentences containing three or four simple words she understands and that are familiar to her upon sight.

Ideas For Activities:

- Make up stories about what's happening in pictures as you look through a photo album together.

- Take a bunch of random pictures, develop them, and use them as "illustrations" in a storybook the two of you write together.

- Have a Scavenger Hunt!
  - Make a list of what you intend to hide. Make a copy of this list for your daughter.
  - As you hide items on the list, write each hiding place on your list incase your memory fails you.
  - Think up clever clues for each item, as well as each hiding place.
  - Pick up a fun prize or a yummy treat to give her at the end.

Real Life Reflections: "When my daughter was five, she loved hearing stories but she didn't like the idea of learning how to read the words on the pages. We encouraged her to read using those books that have buttons you can push that make sounds or play music. She was allowed to push a button whenever she read a simple word correctly. We found a lot of these types of books at the library, so we were able to encourage her to read a variety of words without getting bored." – Stanley, Tampa, Florida

Month fifty-one

"The child supplies the power but the parents have to do the steering." -- Benjamin Spock, *Dr. Spock's Baby and Child Care*

What to Expect:

- She'll start telling stories about what she's done and who she's met more often and in more detail.

- She'll understand explanations better and remember them longer.

- Her verbal skills will further develop.

Developmental Tips:

- Help your daughter develop story telling skills and imagination development by drawing pictures with her and asking her to write as much of the story at the bottom of the page as she can. Help her with words she can't spell, or encourage her to sound out as much of the word as she can.

- Your daughter is going to be interested in how things grow, so develop this interest further by planting vegetable seeds in milk cartons or other small containers on the window sill.

- Bring your daughter to the library at least once per week, if your schedule permits, to develop her ability to pick out what she knows she can read and books she is interested in exploring.

Ideas For Activities:

- Take turns placing items into a pillow case one at a time and having each other guess what is in there.

- Try finding pictures, not necessary constellations, in the stars.

- Have a Block Building Competition:

- Gather as many wooden blocks as you can find that are all the same size. They don't have to be the same color.

- Divide the blocks in half between you and our daughter evenly.

- Start stacking your blocks one by one on top of each other carefully. Encourage your daughter to do the same with her pile of blocks.

- See who can build a tower without it falling down first, but don't keep score. When one of them falls, simply say, "okay, let's try again to get them higher!"

Real Life Reflections: "Whenever we took our daughter to the grocery store (or if I had to bring her by myself), she would freak out if she didn't get whatever she wanted for cereal or other kinds of junk food. We thought about leaving her with a babysitter during these errands, but then we used the opportunity to each her that she wouldn't get her way with that kind of behavior. It was a loud and very hard lesson to teach her, but she eventually understood that we

> were the parents and she needed to listen (and get over herself!)." – Brandon, Vancouver

Month fifty-two

"Fatherhood is pretending the present you love the most is soap-on-a-rope." -- Bill Cosby

What to Expect:

- Her imagination and creativity will grow throughout the year.

- She'll probably try telling jokes or doing things more often to make people laugh or get a reaction.

- She'll start learning more words, as well as their meanings.

Developmental Tips:

- Surround your daughter with a lot of art supplies she can easily access to develop her desire to create often, and to experiment with different kinds of materials.
- Help your daughter further develop her sense of humor by getting joke books that are age appropriate from the library.
- Help your daughter further develop her vocabulary by purchasing and utilizing a picture dictionary often (this will help her read new words, and give her a resource for looking up words she wants to spell without your help).

Ideas For Activities:

- Have ball races by rolling them down a slide and see whose ball reaches the bottom of the slide first.

- The next time you're reading a book together, ask your daughter to pick out a certain object (like how many trees she can find) to find throughout the book.

- Oops! Daddy Fell Down!
    - Take your daughter to the park and, when she wants to go the swings the game begins.
    - Stand in front of her and push her by her feet until she's able to make the swing go on her own.

- Step back a bit so her feet barely touch you. When she just barely touches you, pretend she's knocked you down in a very dramatic way.

- Jump up quickly (or as quickly as you can) and say, "Daddy fell down! Look who needs to be more careful!" (Or something along those lines.) Then, do it again. You'll be met with a lot of laughter!

> **Real Life Reflections:** "I couldn't get my daughter to stop drawing on the walls in the living room, so I gave in and hung large pieces of dry erase board and butcher paper. The butcher paper acted as art we'd enjoy all the time and the dry erase boards were for scribbles that were on the fly. This worked in a way I hadn't anticipated because, before long, those were the only areas she'd draw. I would shrink the space down until we were eventually down to one small dry erase board over her art table." – Victor, UK

Month fifty-three

"When my kids become wild and unruly, I use a nice, safe playpen. When they're finished, I climb out." -- Erma Bombeck

What to Expect:

- She'll probably be more comfortable being dropped off at daycare, or at babysitters.

- She may be ready emotionally and intellectually for a pre-school program.

- She'll probably start sitting to work on puzzles or working with crayons and paper for longer periods of time.

Developmental Tips:

- Develop your daughter's need and desire to interact with her peers by bringing her to playgroups, reading time at the library, parks, and preschool programs.

- Help your daughter develop patience by giving her simple challenges, like making patterns, and then gradually advancing her to ones that are more difficult.

- Encourage you daughter to finish working on one project before moving on to another, further developing her ability to sit and work on things for longer periods of time.

Ideas For Activities:

- Talk to your daughter about what she liked most about her day, and what she hopes will happen tomorrow (then, the next day, ask her if it really did happen).

- When reading to your daughter, stop the book mid-way through and ask her to make up the rest of the story – then, finish reading the story and see how close she came!

- Make a Wagon Truck:

    o Gather all your supplies and place them right into the wagon. You'll need cardboard, scissors, crayons (or markers), and duct tape.

    o Cut the cardboard so it resembles the shape of a truck, and duct tape it to the wagon.
    o Ask your daughter to decorate the cardboard to look like any kind of truck she likes.

- Consider using small tin cans as headlights, a larger can as a CB radio, and sardine cans as taillights.

> **Real Life Reflections:** "Milestones aren't everything. Obviously you shouldn't ignore it if your child misses a lot of them, but sometimes they just don't mean a thing. For whatever reason, my firstborn was on the very latest end of every age range for practically everything. She crawled at eleven months and was so slow to hit speech markers, too. Now, at four and a half, she's running and talking as well as the other preschoolers. Go figure. There's nothing wrong with her. It's just the averages are derived from lots of kids doing things earlier and a lot of kids doing things later, and our definition of normal doesn't have to be exactly the perfect medium of what all kids do as a group." – Catherine P. Businelle, Oregon

Month fifty-four

"To a father growing old nothing is dearer than a daughter." -- Euripides

What to Expect:

- She may begin wanting to have more play dates and possess the ability to adapt to different rules in different households with ease.

- She'll express feelings of stress or concern whenever there's a disruption in her routine.

- She might start showing more interest in keeping her toys organized a particular way, especially if she receives a positive reaction from you.

Developmental Tips:

- Further develop your daughter's confidence levels by allowing her to spend more time at a friend's house than previously.
- Help your daughter with coping skills through stressful moments by sharing with her how you calm yourself down.

- Enable your daughter to develop organizational skills by providing her with adequate toy storage, plenty of containers, and the ability to purge items from her room she no longer plays with on a frequent basis.

Ideas For Activities:

- Change something small in her room, and then ask her to find what's wrong – then, let her have a turn and see if you can find the change she made.

- Take turns hiding an object and playing "hot and cold" to find it with your daughter.

- Build Confidence With Strength:

  - Sit in front of your daughter, directly in the path she wants to walk in. Smile and say, "Try to get passed me!"

  - Encourage her to push past you, rather than trying to snake around you.

  - Before you know it, your daughter will be using all the strength she can to get passed you. This will build her confidence, as well.
  - Eventually, let her bowl you over and say, "What happened?" And see what kind of reaction she gives you.

Real Life Reflections: "My daughter never liked getting overwhelmed with toys during the holidays and on her birthdays, so we helped her feel better about these indulgences (which normally came from her grandparents) by putting things away for a period of time and reintroducing them to her gradually. She felt better about this because it allowed her to carefully figure out what she wanted to get rid of in her room to make room for the new toy. When it was all happening at once, she didn't want to get rid of anything and felt more stress than enjoyment about getting presents." – Troy, Florida

Month fifty-five

"You know, fathers just have a way of putting everything together." -- Erika Cosby

What to Expect:

- Stickers and smiley faces on behavior or other types of charts may excite her and encourage her more.

- She may start arguing or negotiating more often, especially if (when) she notices inconsistencies in your behavior and decisions.

- She'll start expressing sympathy and empathy more often.

Developmental Tips:

- Help develop your daughter's memory skills by giving her incentive charts for her routines, responsibilities, and schoolwork.
- Develop your daughter's ability to trust her peers by staying consistent with rules, following through with what you say you're going to do, and keeping promises.

- Give your daughter the opportunity to develop a basic sense of style and taste by letting her decorate Year or all of her bedroom.

Ideas For Activities:

- Play a game of "I spy."

- Make a bingo game, or use one that is pre-made, to teach her how to play the game.

- Now You See it, Now You Don't:
    - Tape a piece of paper on a clipboard or the surface you intend to work on with your daughter.
    - Set out a wide variety of colored pencils. Using a variety of colors, scribble on as mach of the piece of paper as you can with your daughter.
    - Show her how to erase away using a heavy-duty gum eraser. Create patterns, shapes, and pictures in the scribbles using the eraser.

Real Life Reflections: "My daughter used to eat anything and everything we put in front of her, but that changed swiftly overnight without any notice or explanation. We solved this problem by serving the same foods, but cooked in a different way. She was eating food she claimed she hated without realizing it, so we didn't have to worry about nutrition." – Andre, British Columbia

Month fifty-six

"I love to play hide and seek with my kid, but some days my goal is to find a hiding place where he can't find me until after high school." -- Author Unknown

What to Expect:

- You will notice your daughter thriving and feeling security in her day-to-day routines.

- Don't be surprised if tying her shoes is very difficult for her.

- She is going to be more forthright when asserting her independence.

Developmental Tips:

- Further develop your daughter's sense of trust by consistently being truthful with her in a manner she understands.

- Help your daughter develop preparation skills by telling her ahead of time what to expect (for example, "where going to be leaving Sophie's house in ten minutes," or, "Grandma and Grandpa will be here in fifteen minutes.")

- Stick to your promises no matter what in order to further develop your daughters sense of worth, trust, and accountability.

Ideas For Activities:

- Play the alphabet game – ask your daughter to find as many items in the house as she can that starts with a certain letter.

- Play the color game – ask your daughter to find as many items in the house that is a certain color.

- Color Changing Veggies!

    o Set up a half of a glass or water each with their own color – allow your daughter to add a few drops of food coloring to each class and mix the water to a bright color.

    o Stick a stalk of celery into each glass.

    o Talk to your daughter about what she thinks might happen, and then watch her enthusiasm and curiosity grow.

Real Life Reflections: "It seems like my daughter likes drawing her own pictures, rather than using the 100 or so coloring books she receives over and over from Christmas and birthday gifts. My wife wants her to use the books up instead of giving her more paper, but I like that she wants to make her own pictures. I've been giving the coloring books without stories in the away, and asking my daughter to color the storybooks. It's been a good compromise with my wife so far." – Eric, Missouri

Month fifty-seven

"Role modeling is the most basic responsibility of parents. Parents are handing life's scripts to their children, scripts that in all likelihood will be acted out for the rest of the children's lives." -- Stephen R. Covey

What to Expect:

- Your daughter is not going to be interested in staying in her bed alone at night at all.

- She's going to be spending more time with building sets.

- She's going to be a much more agile runner and climber.

Developmental Tips:

- Encourage your daughter to play outside and enjoy outdoors activities rather than staying inside for quiet play time all the time in order to help you develop an understanding of new play opportunities.
- Help develop your daughter's competitive skills by encouraging her to run races and play chase.

- Help your daughter develop independence by breaking tasks up into several small and simples tasks.

Ideas For Activities:

- See if your daughter can identify signs as you're driving along, and then count together how often you pass by a speed limit or other type of sign.

- Make up stories together about interesting or unique buildings or houses you pass by as you're driving along.

- Paint With Mud:

    o Instead of singing, "rain, rain go away," explain to your daughter how the rain will soon gif you the opportunity to play.

    o Get a plastic tablecloth or tarp and spread it out net to a mud puddle. Mix around the mud with a stick (or ask your daughter if she would like to do it) to make the mud gooey.

    o Set out some paper and paintbrushes on the plastic and start painting on it with the mud.

Real Life Reflections: "My daughter has always loved having a lot of toys, but she played with very few of them (if any at all). Most of the time, she liked making things out of craft sticks, paper, or pipe cleaners more than anything else. Our family said we should get her to give her toys to other children who might not be able to have those kinds of toys, but that was a nightmare. She had a melt-down, and was extremely distressed. We decided to just let her be and ignore everyone else. Over time, she eventually started playing with her toys more and on her own terms. She's happier being unconventional and unexpected and doesn't like

---

> being lead to what is considered the norm." – Enrique, Columbus, Ohio

Month fifty-eight

"The hardest Year of raising a child is teaching them to ride bicycles. A shaky child on a bicycle for the first time needs both support and freedom. The realization that this is what the child will always need can hit hard."
-- Sloan Wilson

What to Expect:

- She might start picturing and imagining fears she's never experienced before.

- She will still need to ride in a car safety seat.

- Your daughter may experience some potty training slip-ups and accidents.

Developmental Tips:

- Further develop your daughter's independence during mealtime by giving her a small plate with the food cut up, utensils that are easy to manage, and by filling her cup only halfway full to prevent big spills.
- Further develop your daughter's hygiene habits by telling her she's old enough to wash her own body in the tub at bath time.
- Help your daughter develop adequate levels of comfort by not rushing her into new situations and allowing her to go at her own pace.

Ideas For Activities:

- Make up stories about how streets got their names when passing by street signs with unique or odd names posted.
- Pretend you and your daughter are super heroes and make up stories about how the two of you would save the world and fight crime together.
- Make a Sorting Game:
    o Gather 36 rocks that are small and similar shape with your daughter. Pretend it's a treasure hunt.
    o Divide the rocks into twelve piles of three.
    o Paint each set a different color.

- Paint the inside cups of an egg carton colors to match the twelve sets of rocks.
- Mix the rocks into one big pile and sort them out.

Real Life Reflections: "Sleep has never been anything my daughter was interested in and that left her mother and I exhausted most of the time. When she got older, she'd stay in bed but she still didn't sleep. Family told us constantly to have her tested, so we did. There was nothing wrong, she just didn't need much sleep. She's growing fine, she's eating fine, and she's doing great in school. I guess if it ain't broken, don't fix it. Even if you're hounded by your mother-in-law for hours on end." – Brock, Idaho

Month fifty-nine

"Role modeling is the most basic responsibility of parents. Parents are handing life's scripts to their children, scripts that in all likelihood will be acted out for the rest of the children's lives." -- Stephen R. Covey

What to Expect:

- She may need explanations about certain rules and disciplinary measures before adhering to them willingly.

- You might notice her imitating bad behaviors exhibited by her siblings or peers in order to get a reaction from you.

- She will find a comfort object (a stuffed animal or blanket) to help her alleviate fears.

Developmental Tips:

- Help further develop your daughter's sense of self-worth by allowing her to take Year in her birthday party plans.

- Help your daughter's emotional development by naming the emotions you notice she's experiencing as she's experiencing them.

- Help your daughter's emotional development by talking about feelings frequently, even when they aren't being experienced in the moment.

Ideas For Activities:

- Go to a zoo and, when stopping to look at animals, ask your daughter to "voice" what the animals might be thinking.

- Show your daughter what happens when you use an eggbeater, water, and dish soap together.

- Make Colored Snow!
    - Fill squirt bottles with water and different colors with food coloring.
    - Spray the colors on to the snow. Make patterns, pictures, and works if possible.
    - If it isn't winter, fill a large plastic container with shaving cream and spray the colors into that.

Real Life Reflections: "If my daughter couldn't help wrap Christmas presents, the world around us literally came crashing down. She would find things in her room, things in her mother's stuff that she thought would make a good gift, and pictures she had drawn to wrap up in construction paper year round, so it seemed mean to me to take this gift wrapping fetish away from her during Christmas. I'd ask her to be my tape person, and my bow holder most of the time and that seemed to thrill her enough." – Mike, Texas

Month sixty

"The longer we live the more we think and the higher the value we put on friendship and tenderness towards parents and friends." -- Samuel Johnson

What to Expect:

- She will start asking more sophisticated questions.
- She will start taking pleasure in pride in the learning experience.
- She may be moodier than in previous years.

Developmental Tips:

- Help your daughter's physical development by encouraging a lot of outdoor play, like at playgrounds for example, where she has the opportunity to work out a series of muscles on a regular basis.
- Further develop your daughter's cognitive thinking skills by providing her with games that are more complex and challenging.

- The average five year old needs about twelve hours of sleep, so help your daughter develop routines at bedtime that will help get her bed on time and asleep without trouble.

Ideas For Activities:

- Gather boxes, bowls, baskets, and other containers and try tossing beanbags into them.
- Place a plastic bowl in the middle of a wading pool and take turns trying to toss pennies into the bowl.

- Tear, Glue, and Cut:

    o Gather colorful paper, wrapping paper, craft paper, and magazine scraps.

    o Get everything in front of your daughter with a glue stick and a sheet of construction paper.

- Encourage your daughter to tear up all the scraps into random shapes with rough edges, but be sure they're not too small.
- Cover every speck of the construction paper with the scraps of paper and the glue stick. Take turns with your daughter gluing things down.
- Using scissors or a paper cutter, cut the construction paper into strips or blocks. Use them as gift tags, bookmarks, pieces for a mobile, or greeting card embellishments.

Real Life Reflections: "My five-year-old is more scared of the dentist chair moving than of the dentist." – Matt Dinniman, Tuscon, AZ

Year Six:

She Might Start Teaching YOU a Thing or Two

"A daughter is the happy memories of the past, the joyful moments of the present, and the hope and promise of the future." -- Author Unknown

Crib Notes:
- Listen to her when she talks. This is important, Dad. Try not to act bored or like what she's saying doesn't really matter. Even if it isn't talk about anything that's important to you, it's important to her.
- Talk to her often. She's going to be very interested in what you have to say, even if it doesn't seem like she's really listening.
- Show her your emotions. If you're typically closed off and don't show your emotions readily, you'll soon learn that this behavior doesn't really work around your little girl. Let her bring it out of you.

Month sixty-one

"A daughter is a bundle of firsts that excite and delight, giggles that come from deep inside and are always contagious, everything wonderful and precious and your love for her knows no bounds." -- Barbara Cage

What to Expect:

- She's going to start collecting things, but she may not be as open about it as you might think.
- She's going to be a chatterbox.
- Catching a ball will still pose as a challenge for your daughter.

Developmental Tips:

- Further help your daughter develop good coordination by involving her in sports teams through her school, or by teaching her them at home.

- Further develop your daughter's creativity by providing her with more complex and complicated arts and crafts projects.

- Further develop your daughter's cognitive thinking skills by encouraging her to copy words from books, and then making up stories of her own.

Ideas For Activities:

- Decorate a cake together.

- Make chocolate chip cookies together.

- Spider Crackers:

    - Set out crackers, peanut butter, raisins, pretzel sticks, and a plastic butter knife for snack time.

    - Make peanut butter cracker sandwiches as you normally would.

    - Show your daughter how to turn them into spiders by sticking pretzel sticks out the sides. Then, make two peanut butter blobs on top to stick the raisins into for eyes.

Real Life Reflections: "This has begun my daughter's KINDERGARTEN class! Granted, they don't understand the workings of such things the same as a ten or eleven year old would, but there has been talk of boys and girls being 'in love' with each other, and mention of supposed kisses between said boys and girls. They're, at the very least, aware of – even if they don't get – such things younger and younger. Crushes abound!

Dads need to be alert to the potential these days, and be honest and straight forward with their daughters. My hubby had his 'first awkward father, daughter talk' with our little one a few weeks ago, telling her it was okay to have boys who are friends, but that she was too young to hold hands and the like.

And dads need to remember how crucial their role is in the development of daughters' self-esteem and self-worth. Especially in these impressionable years." – Janna Qualman

Month sixty-two

"Most American children suffer too much mother and too little father." -- Gloria Steinem, *New York Times*, 26 August 1971

What to Expect:

- She'll be able to do things like ride a scooter, go swimming, and jump on a trampoline with ease.

- She'll be copying her friends, as well as big kids, more often.

- She'll continue to try pushing your buttons, despite the fact that temper tantrums are a thing of the past.

Developmental Tips:

- Help your daughter's emotional development by teaching her how to express and handle anger in a healthy way.
- Help your daughter's emotional development by talking frequently about feelings, giving her praise when it is deserved, being the model of kindness, and teaching about generosity.

- Help with your daughter's development of personality and temperament by teaching her how to interact with others socially in an acceptable way.

Ideas For Activities:

- Find a recipe your daughter likes, and ask her to draw all the ingredients.

- Ask your daughter to draw pictures of what she thinks might be in the refrigerator.

- Candy Jar Gift:

    o Go to the store and pick out assorted candy with your daughter.

    o Fill empty baby food jars, or jars in similar size wit the candy. Encourage your daughter to count the pieces of candy before dropping them in, and divide them evenly among the jars.

    o Place a square or circle piece of fabric on the jar once the lid has been screwed back on. Secure the fabric with a rubber band.

    o Tie a piece of ribbon over the rubber band.

Real Life Reflections: "We're trying to get our daughter to stop sucking her thumb, but she'll have none of that. After hearing everyone in our family, as well as well-meaning friends, tell us what horrible parents we are for not getting to the bottom of this problem we consulted with her pediatrician. She said that our daughter will eventually stop sucking her thumb, but the more we give it attention the more she's going to want to do it. So, we decided to leave her alone. We asked her pediatrician to write this recommendation down so we could have ammunition to fight back with when approached by those with good intensions." – Derek, Washington

Month sixty-three

"Those who trust us educate us." -- T.S. Eliot

What to Expect:

- You may notice she's lying more often than before.
- She's going to be full of a lot more energy.
- She may still have difficulty pronouncing and understanding many words.

Developmental Tips:

- Help develop your daughter's self-confidence by setting up a system of rewards where she'll get a sticker, a smiley face, or a star if she performs correctly or effectively.

- Help your daughter develop a sense of responsibilities by avoiding monetary rewards when she does something well, or when she completes her chores.

- Help your daughter develop good organizational skills in her bedroom by giving her lots of interesting containers to store her things in – like vintage suitcases and mailboxes.

Ideas For Activities:

- Ask your daughter to help you put groceries away and, while you do, discuss what foods belong to which food group.

- Ask your daughter to draw a picture of what's going to be for dinner, and then help her write a story about it.

- Necktie Snake:
    o Find a few of your old neckties you know you'll never wear again.
    o Fold the end of the necktie in half and sew it together, sew a small piece of red felt to the point to act as the snack's tongue.
    o Use craft glue to add some googley eyes.

Real Life Reflections: "No matter what everyone tells you, your daughter will be a master manipulator at some point in her life, Dads. Beware! She'll play you against her mom whenever the chance comes along!" – Bryce, Montreal

Month sixty-four

"Good, honest, hardheaded character is a function of the home. If the proper seed is sown there and properly nourished for a few years, it will not be easy for that plant to be uprooted." -- George A. Dorsey

What to Expect:

- She may still suck her thumb at night.

- She will insist on having a nightlight on all night long.

- She will still love her comfort object, but she may start using it a lot less.

Developmental Tips:

- Further develop social interactions by hosting play dates with school friends more often.

- Further develop fine motor skills by writing and drawing frequently after school.

- Further develop reading readiness by asking your daughter to repeat the words you've just read to her in a book.

Ideas For Activities:

- Teach your daughter how to use basic hand tools with toy tools.

- Pretend you're running a bike repair shop, and that your daughter is the lead mechanic in charge of changing tricycle tires and fixing bells.

- Toilet Tube Treats:

    o Gather a collection of toilet paper tubes, plastic wrap, candy, wrapping paper, and curling ribbon.

    o Tape plastic wrap to one end of the toilet paper tube.

    o Ask your daughter to divide up the candy evenly so there is the same amount going into each tube.

    o Tape another piece of plastic wrap to the other end of the tube once it is filled with candy.

    o Wrap the rolls "tootsie roll" style, and add curling ribbon to each end.

- Use as a gift, Halloween treats, or Yeary favors.

> **Real Life Reflections:** "My daughter never believed I worked all day long, so I brought her to my job one day. It was a real eye-opener for the both of us. She didn't expect that I wouldn't be giving her all my attention, and I didn't expect her to get bored so fast. This was a hard lesson for the both of us to learn, but I think it was worth it in the end." – Scott, Michigan

Month sixty-five

"To her the name of father was another name for love."
-- Fanny Fern

What to Expect:

- She's going to be right about everything, even when she's wrong.

- She's going to have a strong need to have control during playtime with others.
- She's going to start wanting to wear play clothes more often, rather than dresses.

Developmental Tips:

- Encourage your daughter's social development by involving her in as many social events at school as your schedule permits.
- Help your daughter develop the ability to "be done" at mealtime, rather than filling her belly to the point of feeling sick.
- Further develop your daughter's imagination by encouraging her to write and illustrate her own storybooks on a regular basis.

Ideas For Activities:

- Gather a wide variety of beans, and then glue them into a pattern on a piece of construction paper or a paper plate.

- Play the egg balance game – see if you and your daughter can make it from "point A" to "point B" outside balancing a hardboiled egg on a spoon.

- Fuzzy Friends:

- o Gather cardboard, markers, googley eyes, craft glue, and several colors of yarn.

- o Cut animal shapes from the cardboard, and color them in with your daughter.

- o Glue on the eyes.

- o Cut yarn into little fuzzy bits. Add glue to the animals where your daughter wants them to be fuzzy, and press the fuzz into place.

Real Life Reflections: "My daughter's mother and I have very different ideas about how she and I should be spending time together. So, to solve this problem, I asked my daughter to talk to her mom about what she likes doing with me. I learned some new things about what she'd like to do with me sometime, and it quieted her mother's opinion about how we spend our time together." – Donald, Scarborough, Maine

Month sixty-six

"What I wanted most for my daughter was that she be able to soar confidently in her own sky, whatever that may be." -- Helen Claes

What to Expect:

- She's probably going to show more interest in fairies, as well as other mystical characters, and want to surround herself with them.

- She might start mimicking her mother or her grandmother quite a bit.

- She's going to be very interested in listening in on adult conversations, and then trying to become a Year of them.

Developmental Tips:

- Further develop your daughter's cognitive thinking skills by reviewing colors, shapes, numbers, and words with her regularly (playing school is a great way to accomplish this).

- Help your daughter's physical development by introducing her to "child's" yoga.

- Help your daughter develop an understanding of privacy by teaching her when it is inappropriate to become Year of conversations or that she shouldn't be listening in on people talking.

Ideas For Activities:

- Collect flowers and press them in a huge, heavy book.

- Hydrate some dry peas overnight, and then make toothpick structures with them.

- Leaf Fun!

    o Gather some leaves (be sure they're not too dry), acrylic (or tempera) paint, sponges, and small containers of water, crayons without paper, construction paper, and stapler.

    o Fold three pieces of paper in half, nest them inside each other, and staple along the edge.

    o Ask your daughter to decorate the cover using crayons.

    o Place one leaf at a time behind the first page, and rub it with the barrel of the crayon., use as many colors and shaped leaves as possible. Encourage your daughter to layer the colors and shapes to see what she discovers.

- On the next page, use the leaves to make painted prints. If she wants to layer the leaf prints, explain to her that the paint needs to dry unless she wants to mix the paint.

- Repeat this throughout the book. On the facing pages, encourage her to write what she likes about the project or other thoughts on her mind.

Real Life Reflections: "It seemed like every time my daughter found out she was going to spend hours with me while her mother ran errands, she went into a panic. She seemed terrified to be alone with me, which I never really understood because she loves playing with me when her mom's home. We tried doing it so she didn't notice when her mom was gone and, for short periods of time at once, that worked. However, she'd have a freak-out fest whenever she did notice she left. It was exhausting for both of us." – Daniel, Albuquerque, New Mexico

Month sixty-seven

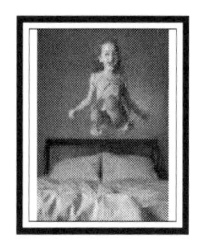

"The one thing children wear out faster than shoes is parents." -- John J. Plomp

What to Expect:

- She's going to probably want to spend more time playing in the bathtub.

- Spending time with family members, like her grandparents, is going to become more important than before.

- She's going to enjoy the school routine, as well as the weekend breaks.

Developmental Tips:

- Help your daughter develop an understanding of a meaningful relationship by giving her your time, rather than giving her "things" whenever you're together.

- Help your daughter develop an understanding of her role in the family be creating a family tree together.

- Help your daughter develop an understanding of where her family members live by marking out their locations on a map.

Ideas For Activities:

- Turn broken DVDs and CD-Roms (or those freebies that come in the mail) into a mobile.

- Have a remote control car race!

- Make Some Boats!

    o Gather some empty milk cartons, milk jugs, plastic bottles, and other recyclables you think might float. Involve your daughter in this selection asking her if she knows what will float and what will not.

    o Gather some Popsicle sticks, rubber bands, and plastic bottle caps to decorate the boats with.

    o Use your bathtub, a wading pool, or a small pond to test your boats out in.

Real Life Reflections: "Whenever my daughter had a hard time finishing whatever was on her plate, I fed it to her. She'd finish without a problem, plus it gave me an opportunity to make some funny faces and zooming noises." – Mark, Palo Alto, California

Month sixty-eight

"When Charles first saw our child Mary, he said all the proper things for a new father. He looked upon the poor little red thing and blurted, 'She's more beautiful than the Brooklyn Bridge. " -- Helen Hayes

What to Expect:

- She will have excellent coordination.

- She'll enjoy physical games like tag, hopscotch, and dodge ball.

- She'll enjoy exploring the outdoors and collecting treasures from nature.

Developmental Tips:

- Help your daughter develop the ability to adjust to changes in her routine by changing things up from time to time in her home routine – that way, when things change at school, it won't be devastating.
- Further develop memory development by reviewing what your daughter learned in class after school regularly.
- Help your daughter's curiosity development by catching a caterpillar and watching it go through its various metamorphoses.

Ideas For Activities:

- Break up candy canes into dust, and then use the dust to sprinkle on frosting for cake, cupcakes, and cookies.

- Ask your daughter to find how many teddy bears she has in her room, and then ask her to name something for you to find how many there is.

- Marble Painting:

    - Line a 9x13 inches baking dish with paper.

    - Squiggle several different color paints all over the paper.

- Roll a marble all around the baking dish through the paint by tipping it in different angles.

- Add more paint and repeat until the entire piece of paper is covered.

Real Life Reflections: "My daughter is a drama magnet and has a way of listening in on conversations and repeating them to other people all wrong. This was causing a lot of problems in the family until people realized what was really happening. We all are very careful about what we say and where she is when we talk now." – Gary, Maryland

Month sixty-nine

"Children are natural mimics who act like their parents despite every effort to teach them good manners." --
Author Unknown

What to Expect:

- She will still show resistance at bedtime, but to a far less degree.

- She's going to want to make more arts and crafts.

- Don't be surprised if she's asking to have friends over everyday after school.

Developmental Tips:

- Help further develop your daughter's imagination by giving her some fabric scraps, ribbon, an empty cereal box, feathers, an egg carton, some rubber bands, and some white glue – see what she comes up with.
- Further develop your daughter's sense of self by making more personalized creations for her room, like painting the switch plate covers or stenciling a border along the ceiling.

- Encourage your daughter's social development by coaxing her to introduce herself to kids playing alone on playgrounds and asking them if they'd like to play with her.

Ideas For Activities:

- Scratch patterns into flattened out play-dough using toothpicks.

- Find colorful "see through" plastic tumblers to start housing your daughter's small collections in (like rocks, shells, bottle caps and things like that).

- Color a Soccer Ball, Play a Game

    o Get a traditional black and white soccer ball, a yellow highlighter, a pink highlighter, and a green highlighter during your next shopping trip together.

    o Show your daughter how the black and white forms a pattern on the soccer ball.

    o Show her how to create a pattern on the ball by coloring in the white areas with different colored highlighters.
    o Teach her how to play soccer with this new fancy soccer ball.

Real Life Reflections: "I love rough-housing with my daughter, but I'm always afraid I'm going to hurt her. I want to teach her how to defend herself and take care of herself when bullied, so I keep it up. Her mother thinks it's ridiculous, but my daughter loves every minute. It's a good way to keep her entertained when I'm too tired after work to read to her or play a game that requires concentration, too." – Steven, Maine

Month seventy

"To be a successful father...there's one absolute rule: when you have a kid, don't look at it for the first two years. " -- Ernest Hemingway

What to Expect:

- She might not be a "morning person" anymore.

- Don't be surprised if you see her eyes start to roll when she hears something she doesn't like or doesn't agree with.

- She might start stomping away and slamming doors when she's mad or if she doesn't get her way about something.

Developmental Tips:

- Help your daughter develop friendships by staying out of the way during playtime, but staying close enough to supervise.

- Help your daughter develop mealtime early etiquette by teaching her the proper way to set a table, and by consistently giving her reminders of table manners.

- Avoid watching TV with your daughter before bedtime because she's at the age where nightmares are more constant, and if you do watch TV help her develop healthy self-soothing techniques if she does have a nightmare.

Ideas For Activities:

- Tie your ankle to your daughter's ankle with a necktie or scarf and try walking around the yard.

- Mix everything up on the dinner table before your daughter arrives and see if she notices what's different.

- Make a Shoebox Collection

    o Talk to your daughter about different things you liked to collect when you were around her age. (If you can't remember, try thinking up some things you might have liked collecting – or make it up!)

- o Ask her if he two of you share any of these interests in common.

- o Get out a shoebox and decorate it to use for a collection. Encourage your daughter to use wrapping paper, stickers, and anything else that will help make the box more special.

- o Each time the two of your go somewhere together, encourage her to take something to put into her box. For example, save some sand from the beach or save an acorn from a hike.

Real Life Reflections: "We thought our daughter was going to be a 'tom-boy' when she was little because she loved getting dirty, playing with bugs, and finding frogs. Now, she still has interest in these things, but she screams when she gets too close to them. She'll yell for me to get a bug, but then will get very mad at me if I get rid of it without showing it to her (at a distance) and telling her what kind of critter it is. I laugh to myself every time this happens." – Stanley, Massachusetts

Month seventy-one

"The secret of dealing successfully with a child is not to be its parent." -- Mell Lazarus

What to Expect:

- She might start showing increased interest in picking out gifts for friends and family for birthdays and Christmas.

- She's likely to gulp down junk food, and spend a considerable amount of time eating healthy food.

- You might notice more loose teeth and she might lose one this year.

Developmental Tips:

- Further develop gross motor skills by encouraging your daughter to walk along a balance beam.

- Encourage fine motor skills with more shoe tying lessons, and by giving less help with buttoning and zipping.

- Further develop fine motor skills by using scissors more often, as well as by writing more often.

Ideas For Activities:

- Put all your daughter's things in the bathroom upside-down and see if she notices.

- Give your daughter some corks and see what she makes out of them or what she does with them.

- Make up a Board Game:
    - Got a yard sale, flea market or salvage store and pick up a game board that's missing pieces.
    - Find a book or instructions online about how to turn it into your own game.
    - Shop for the supplies you'll need for this project with your daughter.
    - Use bottle caps, small toys, beans, or buttons as game pieces.

- Write out the rules to the game with your daughter as the both of you make them up.

> **Real Life Reflections:** "My daughter loves building forts out of blankets and sheets, so I thought she'd love one of those bed covers that looks like a tent. I was so wrong. She was terrified to sleep with that thing on her bed and wasn't happy until I gave it to her cousin."
> – Frank, Chicago

Month seventy-two

"The best of all gifts around any Christmas tree: the presence of a happy family all wrapped up in each other." -- Burton Hillis

What to Expect:

- Your daughter may be more interested in impressing her teachers than impressing you or her mother.

- She may need further enrichment beyond what she is getting at school.

- You may notice her mimicking or wanting to be just like her best friend.

- She might take particular interest in having an imaginary friend, or play imaginary games with dolls.

Developmental Tips:

- Purchase workbooks or print worksheets from websites to further develop your daughter's enrichment skills, as well as get her in the habit of doing homework regularly.

- Help your daughter with memory skills by encouraging her to keep a journal every Monday about the activities she enjoyed the most from the previous weekend.

- If your daughter does have an imaginary friend, further develop her imagination by asking her to use this friend as a character in a written or verbal story.

Ideas For Activities:

- Make play money out of construction paper and play store.
- Tie two tin cans together with a length of string and play telephone.
- Sun Bleached Art:
   - Ask your daughter to arrange objects with interesting shapes on to a piece of dark construction paper.
   - Be sure the paper is set with the objects on it directly in the sunlight.
   - Remove the objects when the sun is no longer shining on them and talk about what's discovered with your daughter.
   - Encourage your daughter to decorate the paper using pastel colored gel pens, fluorescent poster paint, or glitter glue.

Real Life Reflections: "My daughter is now almost six (I dropped her off at kindergarten this morning. ☺)

But one of my favorite memories of her with her father was just after we brought her home from the hospital. When she would get fussy at night (and I didn't need to get up to feed her), my husband would take her out the living room, put in a war moving, and turn the subtitles on (so he could watch the dialogue) and the bass up. The rhythmic pounding of the gunfire would put her right to sleep, and to this day I swear this child could sleep through an atomic bomb dropping. Noise doesn't bother her in the least." – Tasmin21, AbsoluteWrite.com forums

Year Seven:

Be Consistent and Keep it Real

"A daughter is a day brightener and a heart warmer." -- Author Unknown

Crib Notes:

- Avoid sarcasm and poking fun at her as much as possible in order to get her to laugh. What you think is funny might actually be causing harm in the long run (you'll be surprised when she remembers that day you kept tickling her, she wanted you to stop, and you called her a grump).

- She's going to be very funny, so be prepared to capture a lot of these moments on video.

- She's going to be very social, mostly on her terms, so be prepared to talk to her about stranger danger.

Month seventy-three

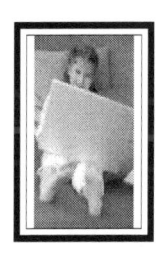

"A daughter is a day brightener and a heart warmer." --
Author Unknown

What to Expect:

- She will start recognizing what individuality is, as well as the fact that she is an individual.

- You may notice her feelings are hurt easier, even with things the two of you just joked about recently.

- You might also notice she needs constant re-assurances because she is experiencing new rejections she hasn't come across before from peers, etc.

Developmental Tips:

- Further develop your daughter's writing skills by asking her to write out all the words she knows how to spell by heart.

- Further develop your daughter's number writing skills by asking her to write out all the numbers she knows by heart.

- Develop memory retention through use of review practices such as drawing familiar shapes, reading familiar words, and dong simple math problems on a regular basis.

Ideas For Activities:

- Turn the food on her plate into a funny face before she reaches the table, and then ask her to make up a story about the face.

- Draw pictures on the bathroom mirror with your daughter using shaving cream.

- Edible Place Cards:

    - The next time your daughter wants to have a tea party, ask her to invite one or two friends to the event.

    - Gather alphabet cereal, vanilla frosting, and graham crackers.

    - Break the graham crackers into quarters, and ask your daughter to help frost one for each guest.

    - Help her spell out each guest's name using the alphabet cereal, and then place each letter into the frosting.

    - Consider creating a border using raisins, m&m's, peanuts, colored sprinkles, and coconut.

Real Life Reflections: "Here's something my husband says that I love, 'I love having daughters. The great thing about daughters is that they can do everything that girls do *and* that boys do.' Case in point: my six year old loves ballet and Barbies (and loves it when dad plays Barbie with her – he has the funniest voices for the Ken doll), but also plays soccer and baseball with dad. She even likes cars and woodworking. So, let your dads know that they should try to involve their daughters with their own interests – even things that don't seem 'girl.'" – MissKris, AbsoluteWrite.com forums

Month seventy-four

"I am not caused by my history--my parents, my childhood and development. These are mirrors in which I may catch glimpses of my image." -- James Hillman

What to Expect:

- You may notice she grows tried quicker and for longer periods of time.
- She will want to read to herself more, and hear stories less.
- She will also have a longer attention span.

Developmental Tips:

- Further develop your daughter's writing skills (printing from left to right, and going from the top of the paper to the bottom) by following through with lessons from class, as well as practice work that can be found in workbooks and on worksheets found online.

- Group situations may be new or uncomfortable for your daughter, so she will need to develop the necessary skills to act appropriately in them. This can be achieved by active participation in play dates, as well as group reading time at the library.

- Encourage your daughter to develop her reading skills further by reading for a specific period of time on a daily basis and mark it down on a chart to keep track of her progress.

Ideas For Activities:

- Have a silly string fight!

- Decorate for a party – even if you're not going to throw one! Throw streamers around play with balloons, and dust everything with confetti.

- Everyday Artist's Stamps:

    o Go on a treasure hunt with your daughter. Search for paper clips, sponges, plastic blocks, erasers, and any other interesting washable objects.

    o Set out paper plates and tempera paint, along with several sheets or large artists paper.

    o Encourage your daughter to collage all over the paper using as much of the shapes and as many colors as possible. Show her how to layer the colors and the shapes.

    o Use the paper as it is for gift-wrap, or book covers.

Real Life Reflections: "I found involving my daughter in martial arts when she was seven, transformed her normally shy,

> reserved, and seemingly dis-empowered persona into a bright, bubbly, confidence." - Rebecca Laffar-Smith

Month seventy-five

"No matter how calmly you try to referee, parenting will eventually produce bizarre behavior, and I'm not talking about the kids." -- Bill Cosby, *Fatherhood*, 1986

What to Expect:

- She may spend more time on projects, show greater concentration, and have a longer attention span.

- You may notice her asking to participate in group activities or lessons that she really isn't interested in following through with.

- She might spend more time trying to master things that truly interest her.

Developmental Tips:

- Help your daughter develop independent work and play skills by purchasing craft projects she needs to complete on her own, puzzles, and other projects that are to be completed without help.
- Expressing herself might be difficult, so helping her develop these skills verbally or on paper may become a reality – do so by giving her examples of how you express yourself, or by reading books about the subject.

- Developing better writing skills is going to be essential this year, so give her plenty of opportunities to practice the way she is taught in school.

Ideas For Activities:

- Take turns going around the table talking about good things that happened during the day, what you're grateful for, and things that made you happy.

- Ask your daughter to draw a picture of her idea of the perfect racecar.

- Make a Button Frame:
    - Go shopping with your daughter to buy a plain picture frame and buttons. Consider shopping for buttons at flea markets and salvage stores.

- o   Set out the frame, buttons, and craft glue.

- o   Help your daughter glue the buttons on to the frame. Use the frame as a gift, or put a picture of your daughter and you in it.

> **Real Life Reflections:** "Whenever my daughter is playing with her friends or if she's around her mother, she's very quiet and timid acting. It's different when she's with me, though, because she's very loud and boisterous." – Tyson, Virginia

Month seventy-six

"Train up a child in the way he should go: and when he is old, he will not depart from it." -- Proverbs 22:6

What to Expect:

- You may notice she fears things she hasn't feared before like darkness, shadows, and cemeteries.

- She might want to roughhouse with your more, but she might be a lot more cautious about it then before.

- You may notice her start to sway away from "boy things" and gravitate more toward "girl things."

Developmental Tips:

- Help your daughter own up to mistakes by explaining to her that she's doing the right thing, admitting to something will not get her into more trouble in comparison to lying, and that taking responsibility is a great sign of responsibility.

- She is going to be very interested in historical figures, and your daughter will need help developing the skills necessary to learn and understand their roles in history.

- Further develop your daughter's reading skills by teaching her comprehension – ask her to explain the story's plot, what she liked about the story, who the characters are, and so on.

Ideas For Activities:

- Try finding pictures in a textured ceiling.

- Try finding pictures in clouds.

- Make a Pattern:

    o Make a grid with 10 rows and 10 columns using a pencil and a ruler with your daughter's help.

    o Ask her to write 1-10 in the squares across the top of the page.

    o On the next line, ask her to put a X in the first square and then number 1-9. Instruct her to put #10 in the first block of the next line.

    o Start the next block of the second line with a X and continue numbering.

    o Ask your daughter to repeat this number pattern throughout the rest of the grid.

    o Assign each number a color, and color in all the squares.

    o Instruct her to color in all the blocks the assigned colors, and to color the boxes with X's black.

    o Talk with your daughter about the pattern she's made.

Real Life Reflections: "I have to be careful what I say to my daughter about things I'm going to do with her because she remembers every word I say. I can't figure out why she can't remember to pick up her toys when she's finished, though." – Tim, Maine

Month seventy-seven

"Any woodsman can tell you that in a broken and sundered nest, one can hardly find more than a precious few whole eggs. So it is with the family." -- Thomas Jefferson

What to Expect:

- She will show interest in how babies are born or where they come from, as well as possess a strong desire to have a new baby in the house.

- She might follow the patterns or her friend's behaviors, rather than defining a line between right and wrong.

- You may want to monitor any ill-chosen friendships she makes, but be aware that they may not stick for very long.

Developmental Tips:

- Help your daughter develop an understanding of how babies are born in a very basic and general sense through use of children's books, as well as literature provided to you by your daughter's pediatrician.

- If you have done something wrong and your daughter notices, ask her what she thinks about the situation and what she noticed was wrong in an effort to further develop her ability to sense between right and wrong.

- Developing an awareness of the world around her may become a reality at this age, despite her confusion about what a town, state, and country are.

Ideas For Activities:

- Ask your daughter to make up stories about where the people in cars around you might be going and might be talking about.

- Whenever you hear birds singing together, ask your daughter to make up stories about what the birds might be saying to each other.

- Seasonal Activity Poster:
    o Divide a piece of poster board into quarters using a black magic marker.
    o Help your daughter write each of the four seasons at the top of each block.
    o On separate sheets of paper, ask your daughter to draw pictures of what she would like to do with you during each season.
    o Glue the pictures in the corresponding blocks on the poster board.
    o Use the magic marker to write what you would like to do with her in the blank spaces of the poster.
    o Hang the poster in her room or in your home office.

Real Life Reflections: "My girls like me to be around, but they want me to leave them alone. They'll let their mother draw with them, but

> they won't let me. If I leave the room, though, they get really mad at me." – Jeff, Indianapolis

Month seventy-eight

"Character is largely caught, and the father and the home should be the great sources of character infection." -- Frank H. Cheley

What to Expect:

- You might notice she brags about her accomplishments a lot more often, which may in turn, make her the target of teasing from her peers.

- She may be a sore loser compared to how she reacted to losing in the past.

- She might start doubting things like Santa Claus and the Easter Bunny as her reason and logic continues to develop.

Developmental Tips:

- Help your daughter develop confidence levels by writing out what she's proud of, rather than bragging about to her friends. Consider making a poster or a memory book to help her with this skill.

- Your daughter is going to need help developing skills to help prevent her from being a sore loser and addressing the situation promptly and giving her examples of proper ways to react to these situations can accomplish this.

- If your daughter if the victim or teasing, she is going to need help developing skills to deal with this type of treatment. This can be done so by instilling positive affirmations, as well as the confidence to stand up for herself even when she's surrounded by negative influences.

Ideas For Activities:

- Give your daughter some paper napkins and ask her to fold them into interesting shapes for the dinner table.

- Ask your daughter to imagine what the inside of a squirrel's home would look like and then write a story about this, or draw a picture.

- Teach Your Daughter All About You:
    o Purchase two "all about me" scrapbook kits.

- Gather pictures from your childhood, if possible, copy them on to paper with a matter finish.
- Gather pictures from your daughter's baby years up to her current age, and copy them on to paper with a matte finish.
- Find multi-colored gel pens, glitter pens, and sparkly crayons at a craft store or in an office supply store.
- Ask your daughter to fill out your book "interview style" and then you fill out her book with her.
- Take turns coloring and decorating each book.
- Talk about the similarities and differences in your childhoods.

Real Life Reflections: "My daughter likes that I let her paint my fingernails, put bows in my hair, spray me with glitter, and do make-up on my face. I won't tell my buddies I play with my girl like this, though, because they'll never let me live it down. Even though it embarrasses me, I

> still like letting her do that." – Dave, South Carolina

Month seventy-nine

"My dear father; my dear friend; the best and wisest man I ever knew, who taught me many lessons and showed me many things as we went together along the country by-ways" -- Sarah Orne Jewett

What to Expect:

- You might notice her saying she's too old for crayons, and would rather use markers or colored pencils.

- She will want to work with paper – making everything from paper airplanes to paper dolls – a lot more often.

- She will want to use scissors, tape, and glue a lot more often – even if she isn't sure what she's making.

Developmental Tips:

- Follow your daughter's creative development as she moves from one type of art supply to another.

- Help your daughter further develop her imagination as she creates new things by asking her questions, guessing what she's making, and offering suggestions to make new things.

- Further develop your daughter's reading skills with her by reading familiar books frequently, as well as introducing her to new ones from time to time.

Ideas For Activities:

- Tell your daughter something you liked to do when you were her age, and ask her if she'd like to do this.

- Put together a picnic lunch together, and then head to the back yard to have a picnic together. Pretend you're somewhere else and see what she comes up with.

- Make a "Together" Journal:

    o Pick out a pretty journal or notebook during a special shopping trip with your daughter.

- At the end of the day, write with your daughter in the journal about your shopping trip and any other activities from the day. Don't forget to date the entry.

- Write in this journal together each day the two of you spend time together.

- Encourage your daughter to draw pictures and paste in mementos, and then add labels to them about special moments from the day.

> **Real Life Reflections:** "I thought there was something wrong with my daughter because she always wanted to be by herself. She never wanted to play with her friends, she never wanted to visit her grandmother, and she didn't come out of her room very much. My friends said it was something I should be thankful for because she wasn't 'high maintenance,' but it still felt strange. She grew out of it eventually, but it still stays in the back of my mind because I don't know if she'll get like that again." – Eric, Portland, Oregon

Month eighty

"Parents can tell but never teach, unless they practice what they preach." -- Arnold Glasow

What to Expect:

- She will start feeling much closer to those around her, both friends and family.

- She might start noticing Mommy and Daddy are different people, as well as start pointing those differences out.

- She may be more self-conscious, particularly when trying new things and meeting new people.

Developmental Tips:

- Help your daughter develop stronger family relationships through letter writing, phone calls, and sending them art projects.
- Your daughter is going to need help with shyness, particularly if she's already the quiet type, so helping her develop social skills are going to be constant. Do so by continuously introducing your daughter to new people, new

environments, and new situations whenever possible.

- Try eating all your meals together as a family to help your daughter develop feelings of security.

Ideas For Activities:

- Ask your daughter if she can figure out how alike and how different she is from you.

- During mealtime or snack time, make up funny names for foods with your daughter.

- Make a Family Phonebook:

    o Plan for this activity ahead of time by asking friends and family members to give or send you one picture of them or their family. Once all of the pictures have been gathered, you're ready to begin.

    o Place pictures in the left side of each two-page spread of a small photo album.

    o On the front page, ask your daughter to write "My Family Phonebook" or something similar, and then decorate the page.

    o On all the pages opposite the pictures, ask your daughter to write their name, their address, and their phone number (their birthday, too, if you know it) with your help.

Encourage her to decorate these pages, as well.

Real Life Reflections: "She hates writing, but she loves reading. She hates drawing, but she loves painting. She hates watching sports, but she loves playing sports. She's growing into being her own person well, I think." – Don, New Hampshire

Month eighty-one

"I looked on child rearing not only as a work of love and duty but as a profession that was fully interesting and challenging as any honorable profession in the world and one that demanded the best that I could bring to it."
-- Rose Kennedy

What to Expect:

- She's going to want to work in more detail with her writing and drawing.

- Don't be surprised if she gets very upset with you for throwing away boxes, toilet paper tubes, egg cartons and anything else she can make things out of.

- She may not like playing alone anymore.

Developmental Tips:

- Further develop your daughter's imagination by picking up a book that teaches her how to make things out of household items that are typically thrown away.

- Further develop your daughter's reading skills by Yearicipating in book fairs, book clubs, and book orders as much as your budget allows.

- Further develop your daughter's gross motor skills by giving her plenty of opportunities to ride her bike, play basketball, run around, play baseball, and Yearake in other outdoor activities.

Ideas For Activities:

- Ask your daughter to guess what your favorite foods, movies, songs, and so on are – then try guessing what her favorite things are. Keep track on paper and then pay the game again in a week to see how much each of you remember.

- The next time you're watching your daughter's favorite movie with her, stop it midway and ask her to make up a completely different ending.

- Teach your daughter how to hang a picture on the wall using a small level.

- Make a Record Book:

    o Go on a shopping trip with your daughter and pick out a journal or blank sketchbook with heavyweight paper.

    o Divide the book into five sections, and mark each section with a paperclip.

    o Ask your daughter to decorate the title page with "My Record Book" or something similar and the date.

    o Ask your daughter to decorate each section's title page, and date them one year aYear.

    o Divide each section into twelve months and ask your daughter to writ the name o each month at the top of each month's section.

    o Ask your daughter to decorate the pages for each month.

    o Within each section, record her height, weight, and other milestone moments each month (like shoe size, clothing size, teeth lost, etc.).

Real Life Reflections: "My girls constantly asks why we aren't having any more kids (she has an older and a younger brother) and can't understand that her mom and I think what we have is enough. We tried giving her a baby doll, and that didn't work. We tried giving her a kitten, and that didn't work. I'm not giving her a baby, my foot is down on that one." – Michael, New York

Month eighty-two

"A child enters your home and for the next twenty years makes so much noise you can hardly stand it. The child depart, leaving the house so silent you think you are going mad." -- John Andrew Holmes

What to Expect:

- She may show less interest in having her hair put into cute styles with barrettes and bows.

- Don't be surprised if she says she's bored and, no matter how many suggestions she hears, she can't find anything "good" to do.

- She may start showing resistance at reading time.

Developmental Tips:

- Your daughter may already be receiving homework at this age, so help her develop a healthy homework routine and be sure either your or her mother is present while she's working.

- Your daughter may already be experiencing crushes, so helping her develop an understanding of these feelings in an open and healthy way is extremely important – dismissing these feelings now will only cause problems in the future.

- Further develop your daughter's fine motor skills and cognitive skills by introducing her to musical instruments.

Ideas For Activities:

- Teach your daughter how to change batteries in her toys or remote controls with supervision.

- Fly a remote control airplane with your daughter at the park.

- Make an Instrument:

    o The next time you empty a coffee can with a lid, or another other container that isn't glass, save it aside.

    o Gather some objects like jingling bells, bottle caps, beans, pennies, buttons, and things like that.

    o Place everything in front of your daughter and let her pick what she'd like to have in the instrument.

    o Experiment with all the different sounds made from the handmade instrument.

> **Real Life Reflections:** "Why do girls seem to know everything, even when they don't? No matter what my daughter and I talk about, she's right and I'm wrong. Is this early preparation for when she's married? It feels like I'm talking to me wife because I'm never right with her, either!" – Chris, Texas

Month eighty-three

"A child's job is to test her boundaries, a parent's is to see that she survives the test." -- Dr. Roger MacDonald

What to Expect:

- Your daughter is going to be more out-spoken about what she thinks is fair and what is unfair more often.

- She might start challenging rules that have always been in place.

- Despite instilling good habits in the past, don't be surprised if she starts forgetting to brush her teeth and hair.

Developmental Tips:

- Further develop your daughter's need to be creative by encourage her to make gifts as often as possible.
- Further develop your daughter's social development by encouraging her to write letters to friends that have moved away.

- Further develop your daughter's cognitive thinking skills by showing her how to look up words she doesn't know how to spell in a "frequently used words" spelling dictionary.

Ideas For Activities:

- Get a plain white paper tablecloth and, while dinner is cooking, draw pictures all over the tablecloth with your daughter.

- Make a calendar page with your daughter, and draw small pictures on all the special days throughout the month.

- Stick People:
    - Gather some construction paper, Popsicle sticks or craft sticks, markers, and white glue.
    - Cut clothing shapes from the construction paper, making a front and back for each piece of clothing.
    - Cut out a head, hands, and feet from the construction paper.
    - Glue everything to the Popsicle sticks.
    - Draw on and decorate them using the markers.

o Play with the stick people with your daughter.

> **Real Life Reflections:** "My daughter plays very well with her brother, but she always says she hates boys. I hope she keeps hating boys until she's thirty." – Timothy, Montana

Month eighty-four

"Parents are not interested in justice; they are interested in quiet." -- Bill Cosby

What to Expect:

- She's going to want to hear explanations for everything – saying, "Because I said so," isn't going to work anymore.

- She might want to start dressing like her mother.

- She's going to start resisting picking up after herself, if she hasn't already by now.

Developmental Tips:

- Further develop healthy eating habits by avoiding fast food as much as you can, and by introducing new twists to old meals so she doesn't get bored.
- Further develop your daughter's self-esteem by starting early dating rituals with her where the two of you get all dressed up and have some special time together outside of the house.

- Further develop her fine motor skills by teaching her how to wrap a gift, and then letting her do it without help.

Ideas For Activities:

- Try making a Frisbee out of paper plates.

- Try making a sled out of a large box.

- Create Painted Tiles:

    o Find some plain ceramic tiles remnants in the discount bin of a home improvement or paint supply store.

- Gather some acrylic paint, acrylic spray fixative, paintbrushes, craft glue, beads, sequins, and gems.

- Paint the tiles with your daughter using any pattern or pictures that inspires the both of you.

- Spray down the tiles once the paint has dried in a very well ventilated area.

- Use the craft glue to further embellish the tiles with gems, sequins, and beads.

Real Life Reflections: "It's really hard for my daughter and I to find things we like in common. So far, we figured out we like breaking things and trying to get them back together again. Her mom doesn't like that very much, but it's working for now. I want to spend time with her and if this is what I have to do until we can figure out what else is going to work, that's what I'm going to do. I just hope she doesn't get bored with me!" – Dan, Georgia

Year Eight:

Follow-Through, You Know What to Do

"I have three daughters and I find as a result I played King Lear almost without rehearsal." -- Peter Ustinov

Crib Notes:
- If you hated school when you were growing up, you're going to have to pretend to love it now – or else your daughter will hate it, too.
- If you hate your job, don't express this in front of you daughter or the fact that you'd rather stay home all day – she's learning subtle clues about work ethics now, believe it or not!

- Avoid being vocal about your dislike for family members or members of your neighborhood, or else your daughter will mirror these feelings – she's learning early cues about judgments from everyone around her, but mostly you because you're her hero.

Month eighty-five

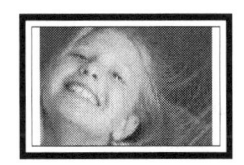

"A daughter is a miracle that never ceases to be miraculous...full of beauty and forever beautiful...loving and caring and truly amazing." -- Deanna Beisser

What to Expect:

- If she has siblings, you'll notice her wanting privacy and wanting to play by herself more often.

- She will not want you anywhere around when it's time for a bath or to change her clothes.

- She may talk more often of her fear of acceptance.

Developmental Tips:

- There are a number of children's books focusing on various fears and how to develop the ability to conquer them – keep these books handy for when these topics arise and read them with your daughter.

- Help your daughter develop modesty by giving her space and privacy whenever she's changing or taking a bath – this will help with her feelings of discomfort and trust, as well.

- Encourage the development of good habits by setting up a bedtime routine that includes washing her face, brushing her teeth, brushing her hair, putting away her dirty laundry, and picking up toys she's finished playing with.

Ideas For Activities:

- Play "20 questions" about what is going to be served for dessert.

- Play "20 questions" about what is going to happen next during the day.

- Sand Art Jars:

- Gather several small containers, powdered tempera paint, sand, shells, polished river rock, marbles, and a jar with a lid for each of you.

- Ask your daughter to put different color powered tempera paint into each container. Add some sand and mix it up with a plastic spoon or Popsicle stick.
- Pour a 1-inch layer of sand in the bottom of the jar.

- Add shells or a layer of one of the other objects so they show well on the edge of the glass.

- Repeat until the jar is full.

- Replace the lid and display them in your daughter's room.

Real Life Reflections: "We found a special place where we like to walk to, and then sit and talk. She's so young now, but it's still our special place. My dream is that she's still walking her with me, as she grows older and more mature to talk about life, problems, and advice. That would be great." – Eugene, New Hampshire

Month eighty-six

"Your responsibility as a parent is not as great as you might imagine. You need not supply the world with the next conqueror of disease or major motion-picture star. If your child simply grows up to be someone who does not use the word "collectible" as a noun, you can consider yourself an unqualified success." -- Fran Lebowitz, "Parental Guidance," Social Studies, 1981

What to Expect:

- This is the first year she will be experiencing puberty in the weakest form of hormonal changes.

- She may be able to tell time better, as well as expect a lot of recognition for being able to do so.

- This is a good year to check to see if your daughter needs glasses because her eyes are changing so much.

Developmental Tips:

- Help your daughter develop her ability to tell time by giving her a clock that isn't digital and teaching her how to use that one on a daily basis.

- Your daughter is going to want to try new things, like making jewelry and things like that, so help her develop these talents and interests by supplying her what she needs and working on these projects with her.

- Because she has an interest in sweets, obviously, help her develop the ability to make them by allowing her to help out in the kitchen as often as she expresses interest in doing so.

Ideas For Activities:

- Show your daughter how you organize your tools and why, and then take some things out to see if she remembers where things belong.

- Show your daughter something that needs to be fixed in the house, and ask her if she knows what tools are needed during the repairs. Then, gather the tools and show her how to use them.

- Button & Bead Mosaic Coaster:
    o Gather some craft glue, metal jar lids, buttons, and beads.

- Ask your daughter to fill the jar lid with a layer of craft glue.
- Place buttons in random order, or in a pattern. Help your daughter with placement using toothpicks or Popsicle sticks.
- Pour some beads into the empty areas of the jar lid.
- When it's dry, shake off the excess beads.

Real Life Reflections: "My first child was a boy, and that was a lot of fun. To be honest, when my wife found out we were going to have a girl the next time she got pregnant, I was petrified. I had no idea if I would be able to bond with her the way I did with my boy. It's been great, though. I don't know why I was so worried." – Tom, California

Month eighty-seven

"The thing to remember about fathers is, they're men. A girl has to keep it in mind: They are dragon--seekers, bent on improbable rescues. Scratch any father, you find someone chock--full of qualms and romantic terrors, believing change is a threat - like your first shoes with heels on, like your first bicycle I it took such months to get. " -- Phyllis Mcginley

What to Expect:

- You may notice her digging harder for answers when she doesn't understand things or when concepts aren't clear to her.

- If she can't remember how to do something or how to play a game, you may notice a lot more complaining or other signs of frustration compared to how she reacted before.

- Don't be surprised if you see your daughter coming home with "gifts" from friends in exchange for "gifts" she's snuck into her school bag to give away.

Developmental Tips:

- Surround your daughter with books that will nurture her imagination and need to learn more, which will help her develop preliminary research skills.

- Help your daughter develop coping skills as she becomes frustrated with things by talking to her about how you handle these types of situations.

- Talk to your daughter about why it is inappropriate for her to bring home things given to her by her friends ("gifts") to enable to her to develop the ability to say no even when she is feeling extreme temptations.

Ideas For Activities:

- At mealtime, ask everyone to switch places and then pretend to be the person they switched places with.

- Sit your daughter in the driver's seat of your vehicle, and pretend she's a pilot flying a plane and that you're the co-pilot.

- Decorative Plant Pots:
  o Gather small terracotta pots, acrylic paint, craft glue, beads, paintbrushes, and acrylic spray.

  o Paint the pots with your daughter following her guidance and imagination. Allow the paint to dry completely before moving on to he next step.

- o Add glue to the areas of the pot where there will be beads, and shake beads on to the glue over a paper plate. Let the plant pots dry completely.

- o Spray the plant pots in a very well ventilated area with acrylic spray to hold the beads in place.

Real Life Reflections: "I leave the 'girly stuff' for me wife, and my daughter and I do 'boy stuff' whenever we're together. We've always been like that and, for our family, it works out great. She plays with her easy bake oven with her mom at one moment, and the next moment she's building a dune buggy in the shed with me. She might transition out of this stuff and that's fine. It's really fun now, though." – Taylor, Colorado

Month eighty-eight

"A child, like your stomach, doesn't need all you can afford to give it." -- Frank A. Clark

What to Expect:

- You may notice an increase in her appetite as she goes through her growth spurts.
- She might grow tired of what she routinely plays with and start to seek out new challenges and adventures.
- She may start "performing" more to younger friends because they make great audiences.

Developmental Tips:

- Your daughter's growth is going to take center stage this year, so help her through this developmental stage through introduction of additional fruits and vegetables on a daily basis.
- Break up your daughter's regular routine through introduction of new activities as often as possible to help her develop the ability to think creatively of new things to do when she grows bored.

- Encourage your daughter's interest in developing into a performer (or something else that she shows great interest in) by providing her what she needs to embrace this interest.

Ideas For Activities:

- Teach your daughter about environmental awareness by keeping the roadside in front of your house clean, and then see if she wants to continue collecting trash along the roadside of the neighbor's house, too.

- Set up events outside for your daughter to compete with you against – like walking a tightrope (which is actually a jump rope stretched out on the ground) and running through tires laid out on the ground.

- Write an Illustrated Letter:

    o Ask your daughter to gather stickers, markers, crayons, glitter gel pens, and blank paper.

    o Encourage her to decorate the borders of the papers using all the supplies she's gathered. Get out some other decorative papers to give her some ideas.

- Find an address in her address book, or in the family address book, for someone she hasn't been in touch with for a long time.

- Give her ideas about what to write about in her letter, and help her with words she has trouble spelling.

Real Life Reflections: "There are times when my daughter is so busy with other things and I wish she'd ask me to play games with her. There are times when I'm so busy or too tired and she wants to play games with me. It seems like a cruel twist to reality, but it still happens. I guess I should ask her to play with me, instead of wishing she'd ask me." – Brent, Delaware

Month eighty-nine

"What can you do to promote world peace? Go home and love your family." -- Mother Teresa

What to Expect:

- You may be hearing a lot more questions about religion compared to in previous years.
- She will start taking more interest in your conversations, even when she shouldn't be.
- She is going to voice her opinions about everything all the time without holding back.

Developmental Tips:

- Bring your daughter to your church (or a local church if you don't belong to one) to discuss questions and further develop your daughter's understanding of religion.
- Talk to your daughter about how eves' dropping is inappropriate, and help her develop this understanding by being consistent.
- Help your daughter develop the ability to discriminate between what should be said and what should be held back whenever she speaks her mind in a way that is abrasive or hurtful.

Ideas For Activities:

- Have a balloon-batting contest – how many times can each of you hit a balloon into the air before it gets away from you.
- Make balloon animals!

- Weave a Tiger's Eye:
    - Find instructions in a book or online about how to assemble and weave a tiger's eye. Look at patterns with your daughter when finding these instructions to ensure you're making the kind of Tiger's Eye she's interested in.
    - Take the project a step further by weaving in beads and charms.
    - Encourage your daughter to paint the portions of the sticks that are still showing when the weaving is complete.
    - Spray the entire piece down and dust it with glitter.

Real Life Reflections: "I can't believe what a little lady my daughter is turning into so fast. I wish I could freeze these moments forever. Especially before she starts getting old enough to start dating." – Hugh, UK

Month ninety

"In spite of the six thousand manuals on child raising in the bookstores, child raising is still a dark continent and no one really knows anything. You just need a lot of love and luck - and, of course, courage." -- Bill Cosby, *Fatherhood*, 1986

What to Expect:

- You may notice your daughter gossiping to friends about what she over-hears others talking about more often.

- She might show and added interest in or worry about money, either internally or outwardly.

- She may require more attention either for you or from her peers – or both.

Developmental Tips:

- Obtain a copy (if possible) of the 200 most commonly used words from your daughter's teacher to help her develop a greater ability to spell, pronounce, and use these words properly in a sentence.

- Help your daughter develop skills for school, such as note taking, by picking up some research materials from the library (any subject she's interested in) and teaching her how to do this.

- Develop daily routines throughout the year, rather than just during the school year, to help your daughter understand responsibilities and expectations go beyond the classroom.

Ideas For Activities:

- Fill a portable snack tray with arts and crafts supplies so, at any time, your daughter can pull it out to work on a project with you or independently.

- Make a bird feeder out of a pinecone and some peanut butter.

- Make a "Let's Have a Play" Box:
    o Find an old steamer trunk, or suitable box with a lid or cover.
    o Go on trips with your daughter to salvage stores, flea markets, and yard sales.
    o Find hates, gloves, dresses, scarves, belts, boas, over coats, and other interesting pieces of clothing to fill the box.

- Try finding wigs, purses, brief cases, and costume jewelry to add to the collection.

> **Real Life Reflections:** "I was listening to my daughter once, when she was around six or seven, and she sounded like a teenager the way she was gossiping to her friends at the bus stop. What was up with that? I didn't expect talk like that until she was in her teens, but I was wrong. It seems like everything is happening so much earlier than when I was a kid." – Charlie, Maryland

Month ninety-one

"Old as she was, she still missed her daddy sometimes." -- Gloria Naylor

What to Expect:

- This year, she'll need you to listen more intently to what she says more than ever before. This will help her feel more worthwhile.

- Discipline is still necessary, but you may find it is less often and less obvious.

- You may see her mirror her mother's moods and behaviors more as she imitates her more often.

Developmental Tips:

- Help develop your daughter's feeling of worth by not being "too busy" or by not being "in the moment" when she's talking to you.

- Help your daughter develop the understanding that school teaches life lessons, rather than just academics, by reinforcing what is taught in school at home and staying consistent.

- Encourage the ability to develop individuality when your daughter start mimicking those who surround her by talking to her about why it's important to be her own person despite how others are acting or behaving around her.

Ideas For Activities:

- Find a very small motor at a junkyard, and take it aYear with your daughter to see how it works. Then, see if she remembers what each tool that you two used was used for.

- Walk around your yard with your daughter, pieces of paper, and crayons. Ask her to rub whatever looks like it would create an interesting texture. Save the papers for future arts and crafts projects.

- Decorate a Lampshade:
    - Pick up an old lampshade that is still intact and in good shape.
    - Bring your daughter to a craft store to find strings of beads, charms, buttons, and things like that to decorate the shade with.
    - Decorate the shade with her, allowing her to lead how it will look like, using some craft glue.
    - Use the lampshade in her room – or pretend it's a hat!

Real Life Reflections: "They always say a girl will always look for a partner that is like her father. I can't get that out of my mind and I feel like I'm walking on eggshells because there's a lot about me that I don't want her finding in a Yearner. Especially the way I swear like a pirate. It's easier to think about breaking a habit than actually doing it. I'm going to have to make some changes, though, because it will only be for the better." – Ken, Florida

Month ninety-two

"The trouble with being a parent is that by the time you are experienced, you are unemployed." -- Author Unknown

What to Expect:

- You may notice her need to have a "herd" grow more.

- She may not be as open with her disappointments with you or situations anymore, and choose to cry alone.

- You might notice her wanting to prove she's dependable more often.

Developmental Tips:

- Help your daughter develop the ability to talk about her problems, rather than keeping them to herself, by being open about certain things yourself and being a good influence.

- Your daughter is going to be settling disputes unlike any other in previous years, so she is going to need help developing the skills necessary to do this. Encourage her to react with a level head calmly, rather than with anger.

- Shifting from independent play to interdependent play may be difficult for your daughter, so help her develop this skill be hosting play dates where you can supervise these transitions.

Ideas For Activities:

- Ask your daughter to write about or draw a picture of what she thinks is happening in outer space.

- Ask her to write a story about what an ant colony does, and what the ants might be thinking.

- Take Something Else Apart!
    - Got through your attic, basement, garage, or storage shed and find an old toaster, hand mixer, an old clock, a broken music box, or something like that.

- Find some flat head and Philip's screwdrivers that are small enough for your daughter to hold and use comfortably.

- Encourage her to take apart the object to see how it goes together and how it's made.

- See if the two of you can figure out how to get it back together again.

> **Real Life Reflections:** "I've noticed that not all girls are the same from my three girls. Even though they're all girls, they all have very different interests, tastes, and behavior. It's a lot to keep up with and my wife is a saint for understanding it all. I count on her to give me ideas for what to do with the girls, otherwise I think I'd be lost." – Rico, Maine

Month ninety-three

"It is much easier to become a father than to be one." -- Kent Nerburn (Letters to My Son: Reflections on Becoming a Man)

What to Expect:

- She may start directing her independence more with peers or with you through acts of anger.

- When playing with friends unsupervised, you may notice more bickering and arguments compared to normal.

- Her need to have one special best friend will grow this year.

Developmental Tips:

- Help your daughter develop an understanding of different cultures through books, videos, and help from her teachers.
- Bring your daughter to a science museum to help her develop an interest in scientific inventions and how they impact history.

- Try to set up a tour of a weather station to help your daughter understand weather changes and, if this isn't possible, get an almanac and explore it with her.

Ideas For Activities:

- Make on outdoor mini-mud track for matchboxes to rumble through with your daughter.

- Decorate a tree outside using items people would normally throw away – like old pipe fittings, doorknobs, springs, tubes, and things like that.

- Go 4-Wheeling! If you're not a "city-dweller," then you'll have more luck with this activity. If you have a car, rather than an old truck you don't mind beating up; don't take the car 4-wheeling! (This is obvious to some, but not to others, believe it or not!) Wait until after a heavy rain has fallen so you and take your daughter on trails with really big puddles. Be sure to take all the safety precautions necessary to ensure no one gets hurt.

Real Life Reflections: "My daughter likes the main living areas of the house to feel like a school room. We have a desk in the living room with our computer on it, so that set the pace. She asked us to hang posters, to put out bins filled with activities, and to have books all over the place. At first, I thought 'no way' because the last thing I wanted to do was lose control of my house. Then I thought about how

> stupid that sounded because everything she wants will enrich her and encourage positive education. I'm glad I didn't let my stupidity take control." – Paul, Vancouver

Month ninety-four

"In bringing up children, spend on them half as much money and twice as much time." -- Author Unknown

What to Expect:

- She may express a stronger desire to have a clubhouse more in comparison to previous years.

- You may notice her wanting to be Year of larger groups ("herds") when playing.

- She might start doing play-acting and other dress up type performances in front of friends and family more often, making things up as she goes.

Developmental Tips:

- Use charts as often as possible as much as possible to help your daughter further develop an understanding for what she is responsible for and when.
- Encourage your daughter to volunteer in the community in some way (see the town hall for details if you're stumped) to help her develop a sense of being Year of something that is not for profit.
- Bring your daughter to a government building, like your state's Capital, to help her develop an understanding for government on a basic level.

Ideas For Activities:

- Set up a landing pad in the backyard (can be anything from an old tire, to a tarp) and try landing paper airplanes you and your daughter fly together there.

- Hang an old tire, and practice throwing baseballs through the center.

- Tour a Paper Mill: There's no doubt by now how much your daughter loves using paper for anything and everything. So, why not arrange a tour of a paper mill so she can see how paper is made? Be sure to arrange this tour well in advance, bring along a camera, and ask for plenty of items for either her memory book or collection box (or both).

Real Life Reflections: "When my daughter was seven, I learned so much from her. I leaned that, above all, be honest no matter what. I learned that it's not scary to try new things. I learned that it doesn't matter what other people think and that I should just be myself. I learned that it's important to keep learning no matter what or how hard it is. I learned that, even when mistakes are made, love is still unconditional. I learned the value of friendships, even when it's hard to share. And, I learned that peas taste better when they're covered with gravy." – George, Maine

Month ninety-five

"Good parents give their children Roots and Wings. Roots to know where home is, wings to fly away and exercise what's been taught them." -- Jonas Salk

What to Expect:

- She's at the age where ballet is desired, and can be encouraged because her muscles are developed enough where her hamstrings won't be damaged.

- She may be more sensitive to smells she either likes a lot or doesn't like at all.

- You might notice an improvement in manners, Yearicularly with others, as she further develops empathy.

Developmental Tips:

- Muscle development is going to be a constant throughout your daughter's growth and is going to have to be constantly addressed and encouraged.

- Help your daughter develop her palette further by introducing her to additional foods, menus and cuisines she's never tried before.

- Your daughter is going to be doing a lot more enrichment exercises at school to further develop her grammar skills, so help her with extra review work as often as possible.

Ideas For Activities:

- Line up cans on the ground, and practice kicking a soccer ball or a kick ball into them.
- Line up cans on a fence rail and practice throwing a baseball into them.
- Make a Book:
    - Fold six pieces of blank white paper in half, and then nest them one inside each other.
    - Staple along the crease at least three times.
    - Color the cover with markers, use stencils, use stickers, or whatever else it is your daughter would like to use.
    - Fill the pages with pictures and writing about favorite things you've done together or things you'd like to do in the future.

Real Life Reflections: "Dads, don't be fooled if your daughter starts crying about something. The tears quickly stop, like a switch, when she hears or gets what she wants. Don't be fooled by doing that, either." – Mark, Missouri

Month ninety-six

"To her the name of father was another name for love."
-- Fanny Fern

What to Expect:

- You will notice less lying, but more exaggerations and excuses for behaviors.

- She may try to act braver than she really is, particularly in front of groups.

- Many of the fears she previously had may begin to subside or become less obvious.

Developmental Tips:

- Help your daughter develop the ability to differentiate between what is brave and what is showing off by explaining the dangers, complications, and problems that could be caused by her decisions.

- Your daughter is going to be interested in reading that is more challenging, so help her develop this need by providing her with her own library card and encouraging her to pick books that seem to interest her (under your supervision, of course) outside of the children's section.

- Allow your daughter to pick out what she would like to purchase everyone for Christmas, or pick out birthday gifts for recipients to help her develop the ability to make smart selections based on several factors (recipient, interest, occasion, and cost).

Ideas For Activities:

- Take a walk around your yard with your daughter, asking her if she knows what things are made from and how they're made.

- Find a really big tree and ask your daughter to make up a story about who might have planted this tree, why they might have planted it there, and who else might have discovered this tree over time.

- Paper Mache Flowers:
    - Make paper mache paste by mixing:
        - ✓ 1 cup flour
        - ✓ 3 cups water

- ✓ Dash of salt
- ✓ Recyclable paper, torn into 1 inch x 6 inch strips

  o Cut a toilet paper roll into a flower by finding the center of the roll, measuring out ½ inch, drawing a line, and cutting strips. Fold each strip at the line to create the flower pedals.

  o Mold the paste over the flower pedals and allow the flower head to dry for twenty-four hours.

  o Place a green pom-pom in the center of the flower head.

  o Paint the flower using poster or tempera paints.

Real Life Reflections: "I'll never forget the first time my daughter, who is about to turn thirteen, made me really laugh at a joke she'd made. We were watching TV and she made a remark about a commercial that had already caused me to chuckle a bit, at which point she looked at me and matter-of-factly said, 'I'll be here 'till Thursday." She was eight. That moment, the look of pure joy on her face at making me roar with laughter is one that I'll always treasure." – quickWit, AbsoluteWrite.com forums

Year Nine:

You Know How, You're a Pro Now!

"Clever father, clever daughter; clever mother, clever son." -- Russian Proverb

Crib Notes:

- If she notices that you're really busy, she'll start regressing and staying out of your way. Some days this will be helpful, but if you let it happen too many times then you're spoiling the bond between the two of you.

- She's going to be interested in talking to you a lot about school, and even early crushes. Don't panic and threaten to get out the shotgun.
- She may assign you as the official boo-boo kisser – avoid telling her to "toughen up" every single time or else she may get the signal that it's not okay to express feelings of pain.

Month ninety-seven

"A daughter is a treasure - and a cause of sleeplessness." -- Ben Sirach

What to Expect:

- She may be less interesting in how neat and clean she is compared to previous years.

- Be prepared for more cavities and the need to be stricter about brushing and flossing as she partakes in treats from friends more often at school and during play dates.

- Don't be surprised if your daughter hates missing school, but doesn't mind being late in the mornings.

Developmental Tips:

- If your daughter is having difficulty "saying no" have a talk with her right away to help her develop this skill – if she's having trouble saying no to treats, it may be difficult to say no to other things in the future.

- Your daughter is on the line between little girl and teenager, help her develop the ability to still embrace her need for little girl things while still being curious about what teenagers are interested in.

- Help your daughter develop a sense of responsibility by trusting her with an important task, or allowing her to baby-sit for a short period of time.

Ideas For Activities:

- When the leaves start to fall, ask you daughter to collect ten matching leaves in different Years of the yard. Save these leaves for future art projects.

- Hunt for acorns with your daughter, and then see what your daughter comes up for using them.

- Go on a Picture Hike:

  o Find a nature trail or sanctuary that provides maps to patrons.

  o Bring a camera for each of you, a small lightweight blanket, and a picnic lunch.
  o Hike along the trail and take pictures of what you see, as well as each other. Ask other hikers to take pictures of the two of you together, if possible.

  o Gather some flowers to press later, pieces of bark, leaves to press later, and anything else that interests your daughter along the way.

  o At the end of the hike, have a picnic lunch (be sure to take more pictures). Talk about the hike so far, as well as anything else that might be on your daughter's mind.

  o After the hike, develop the pictures and put them into a scrapbook or memory book with all her nature items during another activity together in the future.

Real Life Reflections: "My girl is very unpredictable and, at first, that was very frustrating. I like knowing what to expect, but that's impossible when it comes to my girl. One day she'll like playing basketball with me, and the next day she can't believe I would ever ask her to do such a thing. One day, she'll like gong out to eat with me and the next thing I know she's acting like it's terrible that I don't cook for her. I had to learn quick to go with the flow or go crazy." – Andrew, Maine

Month ninety-eight

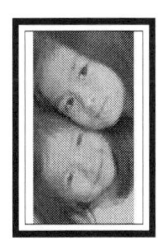

"Feelings of worth can flourish only in an atmosphere where individual differences are appreciated, mistakes are tolerated, communication is open, and rules are flexible--the kind of atmosphere that is found in a nurturing family." -- Virginia Satir

What to Expect:

- She might show some added interest in mythical and mysterious topics.

- You may notice she's confused by common words, but can read new words without any problem.

- She will be able to understand more complicated math problems this year.

Developmental Tips:

- Encourage the development of your daughter's imagination through creative writing, reading, and acting in plays (at home, at school, or in theater groups).

- Help your daughter develop a system of reviewing (with the help of her teachers) because, as her studies become more difficult, it might cause her to forget what she's learned in previous school years – particularly over the summer.

- Help your daughter develop her interests by involving her in book groups, or by throwing a costume party about a storyline or theme she's interested in.

Ideas For Activities:

- Go on a pinecone hunt with your daughter, and see what she comes up with for how to use them.

- Ask your daughter to gather some rocks, then try dipping them into paint and stamping them on paper to see what you come up with.

- Make a Diorama:

    o Find a shoebox with a cover you don't mind letting go of.

    o Gather some construction paper, tin foil, pipe cleaners, pom-poms, feathers, and craft glue.

    o Ask your daughter what she would like to create in the box, and see what she comes up with. You may need to pick up some other supplies.

    o She may ask for some bottle caps, paper clips, and buttons to use in her creations.

Real Life Reflections: "When my daughter turned nine, I felt like an alien had taken her place. Almost overnight, she went from being the sweetest child on Earth, to an emotional, snappy child filled with attitude. When I finally realized that it was the beginnings of hormones kicking in, I decided to change my tactic with her. I taught her deep-breathing techniques to use when she starts to feel frustrated. I also started asking questions and engaging in deeper conversation with her, to get at the heart of whatever was bothering her. When I finally figured out this approach, the tension between us considerably lessened." - Hope Wilbanks

Month ninety-nine

"If you must hold yourself up to your children as an object lesson, hold yourself up as a warning and not as an example." -- George Bernard Shaw

What to Expect:

- She may take extra interest in window-shopping and finding ways to earn money for things she wants to buy.

- She might ask to watch TV more often to help her wind down and calm her mind (even if she doesn't consciously know that's why she's asking).

- She may show a stronger desire to conform to her peers more this year compared to previous years.

Developmental Tips:

- Help your daughter develop skills similar to meditation in order to calm herself down, wind down after a long day, or quiet her busy mind.

- If your daughter is exhibiting a fear to do something because it may be met negatively by her peers, help her develop the ability to do what she wants without worrying what other think by showing her how enjoyable an activity is and so on.

- Encourage the further development of creativity by introducing your daughter to museums, art galleries, and antique stores on a regular basis.

Ideas For Activities:

- Get some dress-up items and pretend you're secret agents.

- Fill an old briefcase with things your daughter thinks a secret agent would use while working.

- Make Up Secret Codes:
  - All you need for this activity is lined paper, a pencil, and your imagination.
  - Write out a code breaker set (like 5=a, 7=z, 3=j and so on).
  - Use the code breaker as a guide to write out your secret messages to each other.
  - Take turns making up codes break.

> **Real Life Reflections:** "I thought I was going to die the first time I overheard just how much my daughter really knew about sex. When did that happen? Who did she learn this from? I was enraged! I got over myself, though, and realized I needed to teach her rather than reprimand her. I asked her pediatrician how to talk to her about this, otherwise I would've screwed the whole thing up." – Dan, Maine

Month one hundred

"I've been very blessed. My parents always told me I could be anything I wanted. When you grow up in a household like that, you learn to believe in yourself." -- Rick Schroeder

What to Expect:

- She will strive toward honesty and trustworthiness, but will argue about rights and fairness a lot more often.

- She may start distancing herself from adults (not just you and her mom).

- She will continue to study the behaviors of those around her to help her decide what kind of person she wants to be.

Developmental Tips:

- Help your daughter develop individuality by focusing on her interests, listening to her fears, and understanding what her peers may be pushing her toward.

- If your daughter wants to isolate herself from adults, her redevelop the ability to trust adults and understand that they're not the enemy (in most, if not all, cases).

- Be as positive, patient, and empathetic as you can in order to provide a good role model for your daughter in helping with her development of personality traits and behaviors.

Ideas For Activities:

- Hydrate a variety of beans overnight, and then ask you daughter to turn them into bugs using broken up toothpicks.

- Glue some rice to a piece of cardboard, and then ask your daughter to paint a picture and see what she discovers.

- Fun Shaped Pancakes:

    o Mix batter as you normally would for a batch of pancakes.

    o Use cookie cutters to pour the batter into and make the pancakes into interesting shapes.

    o Encourage your daughter to do this during slumber Yearies or other sleepovers.
    o Decorate the pancakes with fruit and light cream.

Real Life Reflections: "I always listened to my wife talk about how she needed to go on a diet for this, that or the other reason. I didn't realize this would rub off on my daughter, who doesn't need to lose a pound (she needs to gain, actually). I learned quickly that it was my job to tell the both of them how beautiful they are, that they're great just the way they are, and that they shouldn't change a thing. I didn't realize it was my role as husband and dad to build the confidence of both the women in my life." – Cam, Arizona

Month one hundred-one

"You have a lifetime to work, but children are only young once." -- Polish Proverb

What to Expect:

- You may notice that there's less of a bond between your daughter and her mother, but more of a bond between the two of you.

- She will express the need to be the same as her friends more and more – to have the same hairstyles, the same clothes, the same toys, and so on.

- You may see growth as slow and steady, but your daughter could grow up to one inch by the end of the year.

Developmental Tips:

- Help your daughter redevelop the bond she once had with her mother if you notice that isn't lessened.

- Your daughter is going to want to follow the lead of her friends quite a bit, but the need to help her develop her own style and sense of self-confidence is still necessary.

- Nurture your daughter's need to develop an understanding of how she is changing in comparison to her friends and why it isn't always important to be the same as everyone else.

Ideas For Activities:

- Make a list of ten things for your daughter to find outside, give her a basket, and send her hunting (be sure to choose things that are small and light).

- Ask your daughter to walk around your yard and point out things that have changed – is there a new anthill, a bird's nest, and things like that.

- Create Ice Cream Creatures:

    o Gather ice cream, ice cream cones, small dishes, chocolate fudge, sprinkles, pretzels, cherries, small pieces of cookies, and things like that.

    o Scoop out ice cream into the small dishes.
    o Place the ice cream cone on top of the ice cream as a "hat."

    o Decorate the rest of the ice cream into a face or a strange creature using the rest of the goodies gathered.

Real Life Reflections: "I really thought that, by the time my daughter was eight or nine, that parenting would be less hands-on. I was wrong. It's more hands on. Parents who believe otherwise, especially dads, are in for trouble." – Don, Maine

Month one hundred-two

"It doesn't matter who my father was; it matters who I remember he was." -- Anne Sexton

What to Expect:

- An increase in anxieties and worries may cause an increase in bad dreams, which is typical for this age.

- She may have an increased desire to solve problems, no matter how frustrated and discouraged she becomes.

- You may notice an increased desire for her to plan, make lists, and get organized.

Developmental Tips:

- Help your daughter develop skills to help sooth herself and cope with bad dreams that are associated with anxieties she may be experiencing.

- Your daughter is going to need help developing the ability to step back, re-evaluate a situation, and come back into a problem with a clear head.

- Purchase your daughter a daily planner to help her develop her need to be organized and plan things out.

Ideas For Activities:

- Hang a tire swing.

- Find books in your daughter's collection that are worn out or damaged, and ask her to turn them into art with you. See where her imagination leads the two of you.

- Create an On-Going Wall Collage:

    o Hang a square of chicken wire on the back of your daughter's bedroom door or on some wall space in her room that is out of the way.

    o Each time your daughter and you go out on an outing, find objects to attach to the chicken wire.

- Attach the objects to the chicken wire using florist's wire. Encourage your daughter to decide where the objects should go in the collage.

Real Life Reflections: "When I was growing up, my dad never spent any time at all with my sisters. He left that up to my mom. He spent a lot of time with me and my brothers, which was cool at the time. It wasn't' until I was an adult that I realized how much my sisters needed my dad's attention, too. I won't make that mistake with my girls." – Chris, New Brunswick

Month one hundred-three

"It's not what you leave to your children, it's what you leave in your children." -- Unknown

What to Expect:

- She may exhibit more self-motivation this year, which will continue to develop throughout the years.

- She might start working harder to prefect skills she's already developed.

- You may notice reading problems right away, but math problems may be more difficult to detect as quickly.

Developmental Tips:

- Help your daughter further develop motivational skills by noticing what she's doing and giving her praise.
- Your daughter may need help developing reading skills, which can be accomplished with help from her teachers and the library (or a private tutor).

- Rather the ignoring difficulties developing good math skills, obtain some additional help for your daughter from a tutor or a family member if needed.

Ideas For Activities:

- Ask your daughter to hide something in the yard, and then draw a treasure map to help you find where the item is hidden.

- Ask your daughter to write any letter of the alphabet large in the middle of a piece of paper, and then turn it into an animal drawing. Take turns doing this.

- Let Her Decide the Meal!
    o Take your daughter to the grocery store and encourage her to pick out what will be served at dinner that night so long as it isn't junk food or a TV dinner.
    o Purchase all the ingredients necessary to prepare this meal.
    o When you get home, teach your daughter how to prepare the meal and let her prepare as much of it as possible.
    o Let her pick out what the meal will be served on, as well as how the table will be set.
    o At mealtime, ask her to serve everyone what is for dinner.
    o If time and budget permits, include picking and preparing a dessert.

Real Life Reflections: "There are times when it seems like my girl is talking just to hear her own voice. I zone out sometimes, and feel bad

> about that. I don't give her that impression, though, because it seems really important to her that I'm in that conversation with herself." – Stan, Maine

Month one hundred-four

"It is a wise father that knows his own child." -- William Shakespeare

What to Expect:

- Setting limits on TV, or other activities that interferes with school or exercise, will become more difficult this year.

- She may show more interest in talking on the phone this year in comparison to previous years (and, truth be told, it will only get worse over the years!).

- You may notice she's very attached to rules – especially the ones she makes up or tweaks as she goes along.

Developmental Tips:

- If your daughter is expressing interest only in watching TV, help her develop interests outside the home by exposing her to a wide variety of new activities.

- Because being social is very important to your daughter, help her further develop this desire by encouraging social interactions at home or with your supervision as much as possible.

- Further develop your daughter's need for consistency and follow-through by setting up rules on paper in a place where it is easily accessible to her.

Ideas For Activities:

- Find a deck of cards that is not complete, cut a small slit in the center of each side, and then link them together with your daughter to construction something.

- Ask your daughter to draw her own version of an alien, and then draw yours.

- Little Changes to Her Room:

    o Bring your daughter to antique stores and home improvement stores the next time you're out on a shopping trip together.

- Encourage her to pick out drawer pulls and knobs to replace what is on the furniture in her room.
- If she wants to choose a different knob for everything, let her do it! Try to stay out of the creative process as much as possible.
- When you return home, show her how to take off the old pulls and knobs and put on the new ones.
- If different knobs and pulls were picked out, ask her where she would like everything.
- Save the old pulls and knobs to make a mobile out of during another activity time together.

> **Real Life Reflections:** "I've never been a good reader, but my daughter is and I'm glad. She reads to me all the time. I feel like I should be the one reading to her, but she seems happy. She gets read to by her mom and by her teachers, so she's not missing out on that. I'm glad she can read so much better than I can at such a young age." – Keith, Maine

Month one hundred-five

"If you are too busy to spend time with your children then you are busier than God intended you to be."
--Rabbi Mendel Epstein

What to Expect:

- The groups you've likely noticed your daughter become involved with are most likely going to grow stronger now and become more intense (dramatic).

- She may start using inappropriate language depending on how her peers influence her.

- Her need to have many and large collections of anything and everything that interests her will grow and become very important to her this year.

Developmental Tips:

- Help your daughter develop the ability to understand which are real problems, and which are just bits of drama she doesn't need to get stressed out about.

- Your daughter is going to take a lot of cues from you about how to develop appropriate social talk, so watch your mouth!

- Nurture your daughter's need to develop a sense of comfort through collections, rather than telling her she's just making a mess and filling her room with useless objects.

Ideas For Activities:

- Get some balsa wood airplane kits to build, and then fly with your daughter.

- Let your daughter go through your closet to find things to play dress up with you with.

- Refinish Furniture Together: Because this project requires the use of chemicals, be sure to keep them out of her reach and work in a well-ventilated area.

    o Pick up an old piece of furniture with "good bones" from a yard sale, flea market, or antique store.

    o Bring your daughter to a paint supply store and ask her to pick out the furniture's new color.

- Show her how to remove the old finish from the furniture piece. After the chemicals have been used, allow her to help with any sanding that must take place.

- Be sure to purchase brushes that are wide enough to cover evenly, but small enough for your daughter to handle comfortably.

- Teach her how to paint the furniture, and explain why it might need more than one coat of paint.

- When the piece is finished, let her decide where it will go in her room.

Real Life Reflections: "My mother taught me a lot about being a dad, believe it or not. She was never quiet when it came to things my dad did that she didn't like. As long as I don't do those things with my daughter, I think I'll be doing okay. At least in her eyes." – Jerry, Alaska

Month one hundred-six

"The family--that dear octopus from whose tentacles we never quite escape nor, in our inmost hearts, ever quite wish to." -- Dodie Smith

What to Expect:

- She might be able to read and write decimals.
- You might see her being more organized with her school supplies.
- She might be able to understand homonyms better out of context.

Developmental Tips:

- Further develop your daughter's math skills by printing off worksheets or buying workbooks that focus on the areas of math she's struggling with.
- Encourage your daughter's need to develop organizational skills with her school supplies by purchasing her pencil boxes, pouches, and so on.

- Further develop your daughter's grammar skills by asking her to write out as many homonyms as she can think up, and then putting them into a sentence.

Ideas For Activities:

- Teach your daughter how to change light bulbs with supervision.

- Take apart your DVD player and teach your daughter how to keep it clean.

- Host a Cookie Party!

    o Make some invitations with your daughter using a cookie theme. Be sure to include how many guests will be attending and that everyone should bring a cookie platter.

    o Bake and decorate at least three different types of cookies for the party.

    o Set up party favor bags with a cookie cutter, recipe, and some hot chocolate.

    o Encourage parents to attend this cookie party and indulge in the treats.

Real Life Reflections: "I have a 'daddy's girl' and I love that. She wants to help me with everything, she wants my attention all the time, she loves hearing me praise her, and she loves that I can't get enough of her. I hope we're always close like this. She's close to her mom, too, but it's a different kind of closeness. I think it's great that she has different relationships with each of us. It's special." – Jason, Maine

Month one hundred-seven

"If you raise your children to feel that they can accomplish any goal or task they decide upon, you will have succeeded as a parent and you will have given your children the greatest of all blessings." -- Brian Tracy

What to Expect:

- Don't be surprised if your daughter argues about the consequences she's receiving for bad behavior.

- She may start placing blame on others in order to keep herself from getting into trouble.

- She might want her friends to spend more time at home, rather than going to visit them at their house.

Developmental Tips:

- Help your daughter develop conversational skills by allowing her to ask any question she'd like any time she'd like.

- Help your daughter develop family relationships by bringing her to all family events, as well as keeping her surrounded by cousins.

- Help your daughter develop her social skills further by finding child-friendly events in your community on a regular basis.

Ideas For Activities:

- The next time you change the oil in your vehicle, bring your daughter out with you and show her what you're doing and ask her to be your helper.

- Pick out climbing trees in your yard and – climb them!

- Make Some Ornaments!
    - Purchase some clear plastic Christmas balls with an iridescent finish, and bottles of acrylic paint.
    - Pull the top of the Christmas ornament off, and squeeze in two different colors of paint.
    - Place your finger on top of the hole in the ornament, and give it a few vigorous shakes.
    - Allow the ornaments to dry completely.
    - Replace the top of the ornament and, if desired, add some ribbon.

Real Life Reflections: "Moodiness was the last thing I expected when my girl was around eight. I thought that wouldn't happen until she was closer to being a teenager. When I talked to my friends who had girls, they said my daughter was very mild compared to what they were going through. I knew having a girl would be different from a boy, but I don't like this moodiness and grumpiness. It's hard to stay patient and not call her a grump." – Mark, Colorado

Month one hundred-eight

"Be kind to thy father, for when thou were young, who loved thee so fondly as he? He caught the first accents that fell from thy tongue, and joined in thy innocent glee." -- Margaret Courtney

What to Expect:

- She'll likely show jealousy when she doesn't get what others around her are receiving, even if it's an occasion when she shouldn't be receiving anything.

- If she has younger siblings, she might start acting more motherly to them.

- She might exhibit more patience when trying new things.

Developmental Tips:

- Further develop your daughter's reading skills by purging books she's grown out of and replacing them with books that will continue to challenge and enrich her.

- Further develop your daughter's cognitive thinking by giving her more complicated building sets, more complicated activity books, and scientific experiments.

- Further develop your daughter's imagination by encouraging her to write longer stories.

Ideas For Activities:

- Play in the mud her way – get some old baking pans, berries, bowls, and other old kitchen items to pretend to bake with in the mud.

- Play a game (or two) of hopscotch or marbles with your daughter.

- Dodge Ball!

    o Ask your daughter to round up five or six of her friends and invite them over for a game of dodge ball. If you live out of the way, be prepared to help with carpooling.

    o Head out to the store and pick up some snacks and drinks.

    o When everyone arrives, get the game going!

- o Stop every now and then for snacks and drinks.

- o If the kids grow tired of the game, switch to kick ball or some other outdoor game that can involve the entire group.

> **Real Life Reflections:** "Dads, don't think that you can make up right away for lost time. My father (now that my mother's been in Heaven for six years) feels that because I'm the only girl, I NEED him more. I haven't told him yet, but I learned to live without him a very long time ago. Be there in the moment with your girls and remember that you are the first man in her life. Every boy or man she will ever date will be compared to you. What kind of guy do you want for your daughter?" – Heiddi Zalamar, Bronx, NY

Year Ten:

Isn't it Supposed to Get Easier by Now?

*"And thou shalt in thy daughter see,
This picture, once, resembled thee."* -- Ambrose Philips

Crib Notes:

- Just because she's older and more independent that doesn't mean she'll need you less – she actually needs you more.

- She might start examining your relationships with family while thinking about and working on her own family relationships.

- Don't be afraid to discipline her when necessary – saying "no" won't break her. If she thinks you're gong to be a push over, you're in for trouble Dad!

Month one hundred-nine

"A daughter is one of the most beautiful gifts this world has to give." -- Laurel Atherton

What to Expect:

- She may show added interest in shopping for, and picking out her own taste in clothing.

- If she doesn't feel her allowance is enough, she might try finding ways to earn additional supplemental income.

- She might start trying to prove she is responsible for her own pet, rather than sharing a family pet or having no pet at all.

Developmental Tips:

- Create a "work area" in your daughter's room, in your home office, or in another area of your home to help her develop skills necessary for organizing her time between school, extra curricular activities, chores, and earning supplemental income.

- Purchase books about the various pets she's interested in caring for to help her develop an understanding about what is involved ranging from caring for a newborn pet, to getting the pet vaccinated, and everything else involved.

- Closely examine your daughter's need to change her appearance and see if this need is based on her own developmental changes, or the lead of her peers.

Ideas For Activities:

- Ask your daughter to look through a paper towel tube and then draw what she sees. Take turns doing this.

- Ask your daughter to pretend your mailbox is a house for little people and see what kind of story she comes up with.

- Build a Birdhouse:

- Birdhouses can be made from anything ranging from wood to an empty plastic milk container.

- Depending on your level of skill and tool availability, look online for directions about how to build the type of birdhouse you're interesting in building with your daughter. Print out a set of directions for the both of you to use.

- Gather all of the materials with your daughter, and explain what each will be used for.

- Buy a bird book to learn what kind of food will attract what type of bird. That way you can watch together and shop for birdseed together.

- Try building more than one birdhouse so you can attract a variety of birds.

Real Life Reflections: "I have a daughter who just turned ten this June. She has an eleven-year-old brother. The difference between them is amazing.

My daughter is fearless – but she is not a typical girl. At ten she hates Hannah Montana, she loves dragons and dinosaurs, and she is very responsible.

> But when she was an infant and I was still nursing her, all she wanted to do was use me as a human binky. She shared a bedroom with us and at times we had to put her in a porta-crib in the living room to let her cry herself asleep. Two nights is all it took. She still sleeps with a blankey, though." – Shea Dakota, AbsoluteWrite.com forums

Month one hundred-ten

"The best security blanket a child can have is parents who respect each other." -- Jan Blaustone

What to Expect:

- Moods will continue to shift (yes, this means tears at the drop of a hat) as hormones continue through early puberty.

- For those daughters with siblings, rivalry will grow more this year.

- She may want to be treated more "grown up" rather than being treated like a "little girl."

Developmental Tips:

- Help your daughter develop the ability to manage her mood swings by getting advice from her pediatrician, as well as taking advice from her mother.

- Your daughter will need to develop the ability to be patient with her peers and the best way to help her with that is by being a very good example and being as patient as you can in as many situations as possible.

- Further develop your daughter's need to feel more grown up by allowing her to redecorate her room, or change some of her wardrobe with your supervision.

Ideas For Activities:

- See if you and your daughter can prepare a meal or make a dessert out of food that is only her favorite color.

- Take turns painting pictures with your toes!

- Make an Unconventional Mobile:
    - Bring your daughter to a home improvement store and pick up copper plumbing pieces, stainless fixtures, and small tools.

- Go to an antique store and pick up doorknobs, switch plates, and other small treasures you find along the way.

- Add heavy weight string at varying lengths to each piece.

- Suspend these items from a wire coat hanger, a pipe, or a wrench.

- Hang this mobile in your daughter's room, but avoid hanging it in front of her window so the pieces don't hit against the glass accidentally.

Real Life Reflections: "My sister is nine, and practically since she was old enough to speak she's called our dad 'Best Pal.' He's like a Yearner in crime for her, sort of a confidante, the 'only person who knows' she still likes to watch Thomas the Tank Engine when nobody's home but him. She loves our mom, too, but it seems they but head more, probably because Mom is the one who has to sit next to her while she (agonizingly) does her math homework, etc. Dad is who she pesters to go bog riding Saturday afternoon, and he almost always goes, even though he might have just spent the whole morning cleaning the basement or the garage. He's also the one who provides her with $2 plastic animals and crappy knick-knacks from garage sales. Basically the same relationship I had with my dad when I was her age." – Danger Jane, AbsoluteWrite.com forum

Month one hundred-eleven

"All the feeling which my father could not put into words was in his hand--any dog, child or horse would recognize the kindness of it." -- Freya Stark

What to Expect:

- She is likely old enough to take on chores beyond her regular responsibilities.

- She will be more of a conversationalist, rather thank just a talker.

- She will start taking stances against moral issues such as smoking, drinking and drugs in a more outward manner.

Developmental Tips:

- If you decide to give your daughter chores, do them yourself as well in order to help her develop the understanding that running a household is a family undertaking and that she's not just doing what the adults don't like doing.
- Find ways to help your daughter develop the ability to have meaningful conversations by focusing on her interests and following her cues as much as you possibly can.
- Help your daughter develop a strong platform from which she can freely discuss and debate moral issues that she is taking a stance against.

Ideas For Activities:

- Go to a garden center and learn which flowers are edible, and then make a flower salad together.

- Do you remember your childhood? Get a deck of cards and, each time your daughter flips over a number, talk to her about what you were like at the age represented on the card.

- Make a Plant Bowl:
    o Fill a large salad bowl with potting soil.

- Go to your local garden center and purchase small plants suitable for container gardening. Be sure to tell the customer service representative your plans so they can help you choose the right kind of plants.

- Add these plants to the bowl of potting soil in an arrangement that is guided by your daughter.
- Add interesting elements like polished stone, white stones, small ornamental features and things like that.

- Place the container garden in an area of the home where it will receive adequate sunlight and where your daughter can easily see how it's changing over time.

> **Real Life Reflections:** "My nine-year-old is obsesses with Hannah Montana. I got her to eat something once because I told her I saw on the news a video of Miley Cyrus eating it."
> – Matt Dinniman, Tuscon, AZ

Month one hundred-twelve

"Live so that when your children think of fairness and integrity, they think of you." -- H. Jackson Brown

What to Expect:

- She might show a particular interest in researching, or surrounding herself with knowledge – especially with topics involving adult problems and how to solve them.

- She will become more loyal to her friends and likely to develop friendships that will last for years.

- She may develop the need or desire to start writing in a locked diary.

Developmental Tips:

- Don't be afraid of her need to develop an understanding of what you're going through by rejecting her when she asks questions – censor what you say, but don't dismiss her need to know.

- Help her develop her need for privacy and being able to trust that her thoughts will be kept private by giving her outlets to use like a locked diary, a private blog with a password, or a locked box.

- Talk to your daughter about friendships you've had since your school years to help her further develop the belief that it is possible for those types of friendships to be present in her life.

Ideas For Activities:

- Play some music and ask your daughter to draw pictures about how the music makes her feel. Then, you do the same.

- Play some music and ask your daughter to write a story about what she thinks the song is about. Then, you do the same.

- Make Some Models:
    - Most department stores carry models in their toy section but, if you can't find them there, head to the craft store.
    - Ask your daughter to pick out two or three models she would like to make with you.
    - While you're there, pick up a shelf to display the models on when they're finished.
    - Some models are more difficult to make than others, so be sure to set up a work area that

is out of the way allowing the two of you to keep the model out and work on it whenever time permits.

- Hang the shelf in your home office, in the family room, or in her bedroom.
- As you finish each model together, ask your daughter to arrange it on the shelf the way she thinks it looks best.

> **Real Life Reflections:** "Whoever said raising girls was easier than raising boys obviously hasn't had experience with both at once. There were some years earlier on when this was true, but now my boys seem to be easier. I wonder if it will shift again?" – Doug, Maine

Month one hundred-thirteen

"Children learn to smile from their parents." -- Shinichi Suzuki

What to Expect:

- While there was separation in earlier years, you may notice boys migrating back into the social circles and groups of friends your daughter is involved with.

- She will become keenly aware of how her body is changing and developing in comparison to her peers.

- She will become aware of sex from her peers, and so anything she can to obtain more information.

Developmental Tips:

- Help your daughter develop friendships that are healthy by talking to her about how you choose and nurture your friendships.

- Talk to your daughter frequently about what is concerning her or whatever else is on her mind to help her further develop trust.

- Keep your word when you say you're going to do something to help her develop her own sense of being a dependable person.

Ideas For Activities:

- Get some clear glass plates, some glass paint, and then paint them with your daughter. Hang them in her window using suction cups.

- Get some plain white paper placemats and, while dinner is cooking, personalize them with your daughter.

- Make a Mosaic:

    o Gather the following materials: grout, grouting supplies, glass bottles in different colors, old glass plates, old glass cups, miscellaneous tiles, a brown paper bag, a hammer, a piece of plywood cut to size, and a picture frame.

    o Break up the glass items into pieces by placing them into the brown paper bag and hitting them with the hammer. Don't go crazy or you'll end up with glass dust, rather than glass pieces.

- Attach the picture from to the plywood using finishing nails.
- Once all the glass is broken, start arranging it on the plywood.
- Add some grout to the back of each piece of glass and set it into place.
- When everything is dried, then apply the grout as instructed on the package or as instructed by the home improvement center.

> **Real Life Reflections:** "I hear my girl tell her friends she's going to marry me all the time. She asks me if she can, but I don't know what to say and my wife steps in. She says, 'then what would happen to me?' My daughter changes her mind in the moment, but then forgets the next day. It's kind of cute and funny at the same time."
> – Brian, UK

Month one hundred-fourteen

"Sometimes the poorest man leaves his children the richest inheritances." -- Ruth E. Renkel

What to Expect:

- Your daughter may gain weight, which is normal as she continues to go through puberty.

- She may start being sloppier with her bedroom and her clothes, unless she is met with follow-through from her mother or you.

- Her manners will continue to grow and improve.

Developmental Tips:

- Help your daughter develop an understanding about what her body is going through by purchasing educational materials.

- Your daughter is going to need a lot of follow-through from you and her mom to help her develop the ability to be responsible with her body, as well as her belongings.

- Further develop your daughter's manners by providing her with constant praise and positive reinforcement.

Ideas For Activities:

- Play a game of truth or dare.

- Paint pictures using only your elbows!

- Add Some "Bling" to Her Windows:

    o Find some costume jewelry with large pieces of what appears to be crystals, diamonds, rubies, and other faux gems at antique stores, flea markets, and yard sales. Some craft stores sell these gems separately, but that can get pricey if you're not careful.

    o Pick up some beaded garland that mimics crystals and iridescent beads.

    o You'll also need fishing wire (or heavy duty string), and sheer drapes.

    o Tie the drapes back using a string of beaded garland on each side of the window.
    o Take aYear the pieces of jewelry and string them into a homemade piece of garland to hang along the top of the window treatment.

Real Life Reflections: "She used to get bored so fast that I felt like nothing could hold her attention. I would try so many different things to keep her active and doing things, but it never worked. When I let her pick out what we were going to do, though, her attention was held for much longer periods of time. And, if I let her bring a friend in the picture, everything was fine. I felt like a bad dad at first because I wasn't picking out good things to do, but then I got it that I actually was being a good dad because I was letting her pick." – Jay, Maine

Month one hundred-fifteen

"Children learn to smile from their parents." -- Shinichi Suzuki

What to Expect:

- She will seem to have a compulsion about food, particularly what is going to be served at each meal.

- You may notice you have to remind her to do things or about behaviors a lot more compared to before.

- She will have the need and desire to be "on time" to school and appointments routinely.

Developmental Tips:

- Create a meal-planning schedule that can be posted in a common area of the home to help your daughter develop the ability to understand that, even though she knows what can be expected, it might not be able to be changed.

- Encourage your daughter to make to-do lists to help her develop organizational skills when she has difficulty remembering things (show her your to-do list, if you have one, as proof that it's normal to forget things).

- Purchase a date book for your daughter to keep in her purse or backpack to help her develop responsibility for where she needs to be and when (with your help, or her mom's help).

Ideas For Activities:

- Get some different colored yarn, cut it into one-foot lengths, and ask your daughter to make pictures on paper with it using glue.
- Paint some bricks to decorate pathways and gardens with.
- Make Some Garden Stones:
    - Pick up two or three garden stone kits from the craft store.
    - Ask your daughter to gather some marbles, bottle caps, and other interesting items to use when embellishing the garden stones.
    - Create the garden stones as directed on the package, and embellish them using the objects your daughter has collected.
    - Once the stones have dried, ask your daughter where she would like to place them.

Real Life Reflections: "When my daughter was nine or ten, she seemed to be everyone's caregiver. She wanted to take care of me, her mother, her grandparents, and her younger friends. It was like she was a born mother. Babysitting was never an issue for her, and she was loved by all the kids she took care of. She didn't like being taken care of, though, she preferred being in control of that. To an extent, we let that happen while staying in the background watching closely for when she needed us." – Jared, Florida

Month one hundred-sixteen

"Don't be discouraged if your children reject your advice. Years later they will offer it to their own offspring." --Author Unknown

What to Expect:

- As subjects and topics become more difficult, you will notice her need for more help developing healthy and effective study habits.

- She may become more competitive with her friends about grades.

- Her love for learning will continue to grow if she doesn't feel unnecessary demands or pressure for perfection from her peers.

Developmental Tips:

- Talk to your daughter's teachers about what is challenging her most in class, and ask them for tips to help her develop good study habits for this subjects.
- By nurturing your daughter's interests and encouraging them, you're enabling her to develop tastes of her own rather than following the crowd.
- Bring forth expectations about grades, allowing her to develop a need to be responsible when it comes to her schoolwork.

Ideas For Activities:

- Paint on and decorate blocks your daughter has grown out of building with – turn them into nameplates, picture frames and so on.
- Try reading each other's mouths.
- Have a Lego Building Competition:
    o Find two inexpensive building sets that are the same or have the same amount of pieces in the set.
    o Go over the directions with your daughter, and be sure the both of you know how to build the set.

- Set the timer, and GO! See who can finish building their set first.

Real Life Reflections: "My daughter is a lot whinier with me than with her mother, but that's okay. It drives my wife nuts, but I don't notice when she does it at all. I like thinking that it's a 'girl thing' and that it's special that she wants to do it with daddy. I know I'll think differently when she's older, but it's okay for now."
– Tyson, Maine

Month one hundred-seventeen

"Cultivate your own capabilities, your own style. Appreciate the members of your family for who they are, even though their outlook or style may be miles different from yours. Rabbits don't fly. Eagles don't swim. Ducks look funny trying to climb. Squirrels don't have feathers.

Stop comparing. There's plenty of room in the forest." -- Chuck Swindoll

What to Expect:

- You will notice friendships becoming more complex in terms of fighting, making up, and then not speaking to one another again.

- She may, either inwardly or outwardly, be very afraid of being made fun of or for doing things she enjoyed doing in previous years.

- She may seem happier and more content with how things are going with her family, and try avoiding conflicts more often than before.

Developmental Tips:

- Helping your daughter develop good self-esteem is going to be an on-going process, especially during this year because she's going to feel like she's under the microscope about every little thing she does, thinks or says.

- Help your daughter develop life skills by gradually teaching her how to do laundry, cook meals, and manage her allowance.

- Further develop your daughter's need to maintain a peaceful environment at home, as well as with her friendships.

Ideas For Activities:

- Make a time capsule and burry it somewhere in the yard with your daughter.

- Ask your daughter to write out all the details about what her idea of a perfect day is, and then keep it safe in a drawer somewhere to look back upon.

- Make Doorknob Signs:

    o Gather scissors, ruler, hole puncher, markers, different colored poster board, string, and stickers.

    o Cut the poster board into 4x8 rectangles, and punch one hole into the top two corners of the poster board.
    o Pull the string through the holes and tie a knot on each end.

    o Draw, write, and decorate all over the pieces of poster board.

Real Life Reflections: "She always seemed to want to be with my wife and I, rather than hanging out with friends. It seemed weird at first, but my wife told me not to fight it because in a couple of years she'll want the two of us as far away from her as possible." – Michael, Denmark

Month one hundred-eighteen

"It's frightening to think that you mark your children merely by being yourself. It seems unfair. You can't assume the responsibility for everything you do --or don't do." -- Simone de Beauvoir (1908-1986) French novelist and essayist.

What to Expect:

- Be aware of your daughter's friendships as she enters the age of experimentation. Some of her friends may have already experimented with cigarettes, alcohol and drugs by now.

- Despite how much calmer she is at this age compared to previous years, don't be surprised if she's fidgety and can't sit still for very long.

- She might prefer memorizing facts, rather than coming up with theories or creative thoughts.

Developmental Tips:

- Help your daughter develop a sense of what is dangerous and what is bad for her body when making choices outside of the home.

- Surround your daughter with encyclopedias and other research that is readily accessible to further develop good study habits and her need to research topics that interest her freely.

- Bring your daughter to a gynecologist's office to talk to her about how her body is changing, and help her understand these new developments in a comfortable and trusted environment.

Ideas For Activities:

- What Makes You Happy?

    o Ask your daughter to look around the house trying to find things that make her happy without gathering them, but just thinking of them.

    o Sit down with your daughter and talk about the things that make her happy, why they make her happy, and how often they make her happy.

- o Now it's your turn to do the same – look around the house for things that make you happy.
- o Sit down and talk about what makes you happy, why they make you happy, and how often they make you happy.
- o The next time you do this activity, encourage your daughter to draw pictures or write stories about what makes her happy.

- What Makes You Angry?

  - o Ask your daughter to look around the house trying to find things that makes her angry without gathering them, but just thinking of them.

  - o Sit down with your daughter and talk about the things that make her angry, why they make her angry, and how often they make her angry.

  - o Now it's your turn to do the same – look around the house for things that make you angry.

  - o Sit down and talk about what makes you angry, why they make you angry, and how often they make you angry.

- The next time you do this activity, encourage your daughter to draw pictures or write stories about what makes her angry.

- **What Makes You Excited?**
  - Ask your daughter to look around the house trying to find things that makes her excited without gathering them, but just thinking of them.

  - Sit down with your daughter and talk about the things that make her excited, why they make her excited, and how often they make her excited.

  - Now it's your turn to do the same – look around the house for things that make you excited.

  - Sit down and talk about what makes you excited, why they make you excited, and how often they make you excited.

  - The next time you do this activity, encourage your daughter to draw pictures or write stories about what makes her excited.

Real Life Reflections: "I wish my father would have spent more time playing games with me. He often got home and threw himself on the couch to watch TV. I would end up going to my room to play with my younger brother. Be there when you say you will, Dads. As an eighth grader, there was a dinner at my school hosted where the seventh graders were the wait staff and the entertainment. My mom and sister went, but my father showed up at the very end. If your little girl asks you to be there, be there. Another thing dads, don't use your little girls as a remote control for the TV." - Heiddi Zalamar, Bronx, NY

Month one hundred-nineteen

"Imagine life as a game in which you are juggling some five balls in the air. You name them . . . work, family, health, friends and spirit, and you're keeping all of these in the air. You will soon understand that work is a rubber ball. If you drop it, it will bounce back. But the other four balls . . . family, health, friends and spirit . . . are made of glass. If you drop one of these, they will be *irrevocably scuffed, marked, nicked, damaged or even shattered. They will never be the same."* -- Unknown

What to Expect:

- Expect a rapid growth spurt during this year, but don't be too alarmed if is not as much as her friends (or if it's more, for that matter).

- You may notice your daughter trying food she previously "hated" and no longer being quite as picky at the table.

- She might start expressing she doesn't need as much sleep as when she was "a kid," but this isn't true of course.

Developmental Tips:

- Help your daughter develop problem-solving skills by allowing her to make as many decisions as she possibly can, and then helping her sort out the mistakes she's made along the way.

- Your daughter is going to be experiencing some intense friendships and will need help developing coping mechanisms as well as the ability to choose right from wrong in heated situations.

- Enhance your daughter's creative development by providing her with as many outlets as possible (acting, singing, playing an instrument, etc.).

Ideas For Activities:

- Sit down with your daughter and make a list of five bad habits each of you have, and then spend the next week helping each other change these habits.

- Ask your daughter to look at a picture, and then take it away to see how much of it she can remember. Then, you do the same. Take turns with many pictures.

- Flashlight Chases:

    o Gather two flashlights, and head into your daughter's room with her when it's dark outside.

    o Turn off the lights and sit in the middle of her bedroom.

    o Turn on the flashlights, shine them at the ceiling, and play chase with each other.

    o When she catches your light, reverse it so you chase her light.

    o Keep taking turns until she grows tired of the game.

Real Life Reflections: "When I wasn't working, I couldn't leave the house without my daughter tagging along with me. It didn't matter if I was heading up to the hardware store to pick up new faucet, or if I was getting gas – she wanted to be there. I thought it was the coolest thing because my friends could never get their daughters away from their mother's sides." – Peter, Massachusetts

Month one hundred-twenty

"I have always looked at life as a voyage, mostly wonderful, sometimes frightening. In my family and friends I have discovered treasure more valuable than gold." -- Jimmy Buffet

What to Expect:

- Don't be surprised if your early riser has difficulty getting out of bed in the mornings now.

- She may show additional resistance about bathing and washing up, but is easily swayed with parent involvement and consistent routines or rituals.

- Your daughter will continue to need help rinsing shampoo from her hair, especially if it's kept long.

Developmental Tips:

- Help your daughter develop responsibilities by getting her an alarm clock, and asking her to get herself up in the morning (with your help, of course).

- Your daughter is on the cusp of starting her period, so help her develop good hygiene habits now with her mother's help.

- Further develop your daughter's self-esteem and confidence by complimenting her whenever you can.

Ideas For Activities:

- Make a newspaper with your daughter and, if you have the room, set up a pretend newsroom to work in.

- Play a game of true or false.
- Make Some Trail Mix:
    - Gather a medium sized bowl, plastic bags, spoon, measuring cups, some peanuts, raisins, granola, chocolate chips, sunflower seeds, and dried fruit.
    - Ask your daughter to measure out equal Years of each ingredient, pour them into the bowl, and mix them up.
    - Talk about the ingredients with your daughter, asking her what she likes best and how she thinks it might taste when it's finished.
    - Ask your daughter to measure out equal Years of the mix and pour it into the plastic bags.
    - Save some of these bags of trail mix for the next time you and your daughter go on an outing together.

Real Life Reflections: "Don't forget: even at age ten girls are beginning to act and react to boys the way we did when we were twelve or thirteen. At age ten or eleven my daughters were already commenting about how one boy or other was 'in love' with a girl from their class and wanted to 'go out' with said girl. Makes for the beginning of a very confusing time.

I find the worst thing dads can do is pretend that this is silly or that 'they shouldn't be thinking about that because they're too young.' It's best just to turn the serious, listening ear. That's all the want and sometimes to listen so they can figure things out in the open on their own." – emandem, AbsoluteWrite.com forums

Final Thoughts:

It's Not Really the End . . . it's Still the Beginning. Really.

"What lies behind us and what lies before us are tiny matters compared to what lies within us." – Ralph Waldo Emerson

You made it! Well, you made it through the first decade that is. There's still so much left to learn, but you really should pride yourself for the strides you've made so far. The day your daughter was born, you already started a special relationship with her unlike any other you'll experience in your life. Even though she's ten now, and ready for big girl things, she'll always be daddy's little girl.

Don't forget to seek additional resources (some of which are listed at the end of this book) for the next eight years of your daughter's development. So long as she's under your roof, you're going to want to have a firm handle of what's going on, what to expect, and have some clues as to what to d with her. Especially when she reaches that stage of development when she doesn't want anything to do with you! Don't take it personally, dads, it's inevitable.

Remember, the learning process is seemingly never ending and just when you think you have a grasp on what's going on – something new comes your way. You're going to be learning just as much as your daughter does as she continues going through various stages of development, if not more. She'll keep you on your toes, but that's one of the many benefits of being a father.

Additional Resources

Books:

- *Be Prepared: A Practical Handbook for New Dads* by Gary Greenberg, and Jeannie Hayden

- *The New Dad's Survival Guide: Man-to-Man Advice for First-Time Fathers* by Scott Mactavish

- *Checklists for the New Dad: The Expectant Father's Guide to Pregnancy, Delivery, and Baby's First Year*, by Joe Deyo

- *Father's First Steps: 25 Things Every New Dad Should Know* by Robert W. Sears, and James

M. Sears

- *The New Father Series Boxed Set: The New Father, A Dad's Guide to The First Year; A Dad's Guide to the Toddler Years* by Armin A. Brott

- *Pacify Me: A Handbook for the Freaked-Out New Dad* by Chris Mancini

- *Hit the Ground Crawling: Lessons From 150,000 New Fathers* by Greg Bishop

- *Crouching Father, Hidden Toddler: A Zen Guide for New Dads* by C. W. Nevius, and Beegee Tolpa
- *Mack Daddy: Mastering Fatherhood without Losing Your Style, Your Cool, or Your Mind* by Larry Bleidner

- *Dad's Pregnant Too: Expectant fathers, expectant mothers, new dads and new moms share advice, tips and stories about all the surprises, questions and joys ahead...* by Harlan Cohen

Websites:

- Dad's Adventure http://www.dadsadventure.com/

- The Dad Man http://www.thedadman.com/

- AtHomeDad.org: The Stay at Home Dad Oasis http://www.athomedad.org/

- FATHERS.com http://www.fathers.com/

- For Fathers: Advice for Dads http://www.fatherhood.org/Page.aspx?pid=242

- Brand New Dad: A Social Network and Resource Center for New Dads http://www.brandnewdad.com/

- Great Dad: Advice for Expectant Dads and New Dads http://www.greatdad.com/

- Boot Camp for New Dads http://www.bootcampfornewdads.org/
- Daddy Types: A Weblog for New Dads http://daddytypes.com/

- MayoClinic.com: New Dad: Tips to Help Manage Stress http://www.mayoclinic.com/health/new-dad/MY01094

Acknowledgments

I would like to sincerely thank the following people for offering their "Real Life Reflections" at the conclusion of each Month of this book. Your input, insight, ideas, and advice make this handbook a well-rounded and finished piece. Thank you! (These names are listed in order of appearance.)

- Bonnie Harris is author of *Confident Parents, Remarkable Kids: 8 Principles for Raising Kids You'll Love to Live With* (Adams Media, Sept. 2008), and wrote the parenting classic, *When Kids Push Your Buttons* (Warner Books), a top-selling title that has been translated into a half a dozen languages. She's an esteemed parenting educator, international speaker, and a pioneer of child behavior strategies.
- December Quinn is a multi-published author of romance and erotic romance. She lives in England with her husband and their two little girls. (http://www.decemberquinn.com/)
- Rebecca Laffar-Smith: With over ten years experience, Rebecca Laffar-Smith is a freelance

writer, editor, and web tech who really knows her field. (http://www.craftingfiction.com)
- J. Leslie Voss, Australia
- Janna Qualman is a freelance and women's fiction writer. She lives with her family in the Midwest, where she captures life through writing. (http://somethingshewrote.blogspot.com/)
- LaurieD, AbsoluteWrite.com forums
- Jason, Georgia
- Anthony, Portland, Oregon
- Rich, Portsmouth, New Hampshire
- Melia, Ohio
- Megan, Australia
- Janna, AbsoluteWrite.com forums
- Kimberly Nee fell in love with historical romance when she was sixteen, and blames Kathleen Woodiwiss for that, since it was her *The Flame and the Flower* that got her hooked. Not long after finishing it, she sat down to write one herself and now, many years later, here she is. (http://www.kimberlynee.com/)
- Elladog, AbsoluteWrite.com forums
- Brandy, from Virginia
- Kristy26, AbosulteWrite.com forums
- Kyle, Edison, New Jersey
- MissKris, AbsoluteWrite.com forums
- Monkey, AbsoluteWrite.com
- Craig, Rhode Island
- Gene, California
- Stacy Violette, from Newport News, VA.
- John, Massachusetts
- Andrew, Oregon

o   Catherine P. Businelle, Oregon, has written for several magazines, including *ByLine*, *Verbatim*, *Christian Home & School*, and *American Iron Magazine*. She has also written for non-profit organizations, translated books into Spanish, and is currently working on a proposal for a book of birth stories.
o   Wendy Pinkston Cebula is a story writer currently working on her novel and living in the city. Read about her writing and city living adventures on her blog, http://wendypinkstoncebula.blogspot.com/
o   Elizabeth, New York
o   Alex, Australia
o   Christian, Mississippi
o   Geoff, Washington
o   Phillip, Maine
o   Colin, Maine
o   Erin Yearridge, an art therapist at a state hospital in CA.
o   Brad, Vermont
o   Stacia Kane, is a multi-published urban author living in Southwest England (http://www.staciakane.net/)
o   Danger Jane, AbsoluteWrite.com forums
o   Matt Dinniman, Tuscon, AZ, is author of *Shivered Sky* and *Trailer Park Fairy Tales* (http://www.mattdinniman.com/)
o   Jason, Georgia
o   Bryant, New Jersey
o   Todd, Nebraska
o   Patrick, UK

- Richard, Texas
- Mitch, Queens
- Nicholas, Pennsylvania
- heyjude, Absolutewrite.com forums
- Stanley, Tampa, Florida
- Brandon, Vancouver
- Victor, UK
- Troy, Florida
- Andre, British Columbia
- Eric, Missouri
- Enrique, Columbus, Ohio
- Brock, Idaho
- Derek, Washington
- Bryce, Montreal
- Scott, Michigan
- Donald, Scarborough, Maine
- Daniel, Albuquerque, New Mexico
- Mark, Palo Alto, California
- Gary, Maryland
- Steven, Maine
- Stanley, Massachusetts
- Frank, Chicago
- Tasmin21, AbsoluteWrite.com forums
- Tyson, Virginia
- Tim, Maine
- Jeff, Indianapolis
- Dave, South Carolina
- Eric, Portland, Oregon
- Don, New Hampshire
- Michael, New York
- Chris, Texas

- Timothy, Montana
- Dan, Georgia
- Eugene, New Hampshire
- Tom, California
- Taylor, Colorado
- Brent, Delaware
- Hugh, UK
- Charlie, Maryland
- Ken, Florida
- Ken, Florida
- Paul, Vancouver
- George, Maine
- Mark, Missouri
- quickWit, AbsoluteWrite.com forums
- Andrew, Maine
- Hope Wilbanks is an inspirational non-fiction writer. Her writing has been published extensively in both online and print publications. (http://www.hopewilbanks.com/)
- Dan, Maine
- Cam, Arizona
- Don, Maine
- Chris, New Brunswick
- Stan, Maine
- Keith, Maine
- Jerry, Alaska
- Jason, Maine
- Mark, Colorado
- Heiddi Zalamar, Bronx, NY, is a freelance writer, mom and therapist living in New York City. Heiddi began journaling as a child and has expanded her writing to include articles, reports,

essays, etc both online and in print. Heiddi can write about various topics including parenting, family, education, business, and counseling. (http://thefreshmanwriter.wordpress.com/)
- Shea Dakota, AbsoluteWrite.com forums
- Brian, UK
- Jared, Florida
- Michael, Denmark
- Peter, Massachusetts
- emandem, AbsoluteWrite.com forums

About the Author

Jenn Greenleaf is a freelance writer and author hailing from the great state of Maine. She's been active in the writing and publishing industry since 1999, which happened to be the same year she became a first-time mother. She's now raising three children with her wonderful husband, Chris.

Jenn has also been a commissioned artist since 1993. She began her career as a landscape and still life artist, and later moved on to mixed-media art in 2003. Her interest in mixed-media began when she started actively participating in mail-art projects through various websites. These efforts, of course, lead to writing various how-to and other mixed-media related articles.

More Books By Jenn

101 Mixed-Media Art Project,   Art Journal Prompts & Points

How-to's & Ideas
$16.99

to Ponder
$12.99

While We're Apart: A Fill in the Blank Book
$11.99

While We're Still Apart: A Fill in the Blank Book
$11.99

Because We're Apart: A Fill in the Blank Book
$11.99

Maine Living: One Writer's Perspective
$12.99

Raising Your Daughter from Ages 0-10   357

Made in the USA
Lexington, KY
08 December 2010